"Dr Yasser Mattar sets out the precise steps for crafting every component of a personal brand. The chapters are filled with real-life examples that we can relate to, and he has also given us templates and sifting questions to work on."

— Erica Tham, Life Coach

"I would recommend the book to anyone who is about to start their journey in personal branding. It is an easy read, with everyday examples showing the relevance of personal branding to different kinds of people, markets and industries."

— Ku Sim Ling, Director of Corporate Services

"A precise prescription for professionals wondering about their next career move."

— Daniel da Costa, CEO

REBRAND YOURSELF
RETELL YOUR STORY

Personal branding for career success

Yasser Mattar

© 2023 Yasser Mattar

Published in 2023 by Marshall Cavendish Business
An imprint of Marshall Cavendish International

All rights reserved

No part of this publication may be reproduced, stored in a retrieval system or transmitted, in any form or by any means, electronic, mechanical, photocopying, recording or otherwise, without the prior permission of the copyright owner. Requests for permission should be addressed to the Publisher, Marshall Cavendish International (Asia) Private Limited, 1 New Industrial Road, Singapore 536196. Tel: (65) 6213 9300 E-mail: genref@sg.marshallcavendish.com
Website: www.marshallcavendish.com

The publisher makes no representation or warranties with respect to the contents of this book, and specifically disclaims any implied warranties or merchantability or fitness for any particular purpose, and shall in no event be liable for any loss of profit or any other commercial damage, including but not limited to special, incidental, consequential, or other damages.

Other Marshall Cavendish Offices:
Marshall Cavendish Corporation, 800 Westchester Ave, Suite N-641, Rye Brook, NY 10573, USA • Marshall Cavendish International (Thailand) Co Ltd, 253 Asoke, 16th Floor, Sukhumvit 21 Road, Klongtoey Nua, Wattana, Bangkok 10110, Thailand • Marshall Cavendish (Malaysia) Sdn Bhd, Times Subang, Lot 46, Subang Hi-Tech Industrial Park, Batu Tiga, 40000 Shah Alam, Selangor Darul Ehsan, Malaysia

Marshall Cavendish is a registered trademark of Times Publishing Limited

National Library Board, Singapore Cataloguing in Publication Data
Name(s): Mattar, Yasser.
Title: Rebrand yourself, retell your story : personal branding for career success / Yasser Mattar.
Description: Singapore : Marshall Cavendish Business, 2023.
Identifier(s): ISBN 978-981-5066-70-8 (paperback)
Subject(s): LCSH: Branding (Marketing) | Career development.
Classification: DDC 650.1--dc23

Printed in Singapore

CONTENTS

Chapter 1: Introduction — 9
The person, the professional, the personal brand — 15
The roadmap — 19

Chapter 2: The Conceptual Grounding of Personal Branding — 26
Brand persona — 28
    Personal brand persona — 40
Competencies — 53
Storytelling — 61
    Storytelling for personal brands — 70
Taking stock — 83

Chapter 3: The Benefits of Personal Branding — 87
Gaining a competitive advantage — 90
Staying relevant — 85
Mitigating the risks of "the many watching the many" — 99
Building resilience — 106
Sending a clear signal to the market and industry — 115
Taking stock — 119

Chapter 4: The "When" — 122
Brand refresh — 129
Rebranding — 131
Taking stock — 144

Chapter 5: Step 1: Developing Competencies — 146
Step 1.1: Identify your strengths, weaknesses, opportunities and threats — 151
Step 1.2: Analyse market needs and industry trends — 160
Step 1.3: Empathise with yourself — 163
Step 1.4: Identify performance gap — 168
Step 1.5: Learn — 170
Step 1.6: Practise — 174
Step 1.7: Apply — 175
Taking stock — 179

Chapter 6: Step 2: Craft your Brand Persona — 183
Step 2.1: Renounce the employee mindset — 186
Step 2.2: Depersonify yourself — 187
Step 2.3: Identify a core archetype based on your area of competency — 189
Step 2.4: Identify an influencer archetype that you are comfortable with carrying — 190
Step 2.5: Amalgamate your core and influencer archetypes — 191
Step 2.6: Build up the components of your brand persona — 192
    Step 2.6.1: Choose a brand name — 193
    Step 2.6.2: Create a brand slogan — 197

Step 2.6.3: Craft a brand voice 198
Step 2.6.4: Craft your brand values 202
Step 2.6.5: Flip your values around to see
    your anti-values 204
Step 2.6.6: Visualise your brand visual identity 205
Step 2.6.7: Craft a brand vision 209
Step 2.6.8: Craft a brand mission 210
Taking stock 212

Chapter 7: Step 3: (Re)tell Your Story — 215
Step 3.1: Apply a three-act structure 216
Step 3.2: Decide what to do with your former
    personal brand 219
Step 3.3: Modify the story with an archetypal plot 220
Step 3.4: Add some persuasive spice 221
Taking stock 223

Chapter 8: Step 4: Optimising Your Personal Brand — 224
Action 1: Keep your eye on the market and industry 227
Action 2: Update your digital presence 233
Action 3: Watch out for threats 235
Taking stock 237

Chapter 9: Not the End, but the Beginning — 240

About the Author — 246

CHAPTER 1

Introduction

Have you been saved? No, wait, let me stop myself right there. As much as I am a practitioner and advocate of personal branding, I don't want to come across right off the bat as evangelical.

But I am going to try to convince you of the virtues of personal branding. I am going to tell you all about personal branding and why it will be beneficial to you. I am going to illustrate personal branding using various examples from various industries. I am going to take you through how you can undertake a personal branding exercise step by step. In this rapidly changing business world, powered by digitisation, I believe that personal branding is the way to go for professionals and entrepreneurs alike.

I am a strong advocate of personal branding, because I believe it holds the key to our professional identities in this digital world. No longer should we see ourselves as merely an employee of an organisation. The multitude of channels for our professional voices to be heard and for our professional identities to be seen means that we do not need to constrain ourselves to working within the limits of our organisations. With a strong personal brand, we have our sights set on the larger industry, and we are ready to tackle any challenges that come our way. We therefore should wear our personal brands proudly, as avatars of our professional identities.

The title of this book is *(Re)brand Yourself, (Re)tell Your Story*. Why is that? Well, some of us are about to go on our very first personal branding journey. Some of us are refreshing our personal brands because there are some tiny adjustments we need to make to remain relevant to the market and the industry. Yet, some of us need to rebrand. Maybe we've had some trouble getting our current brands to work for us. Maybe the market has changed. Maybe we've had problems landing jobs recently. Whatever it might be, we need to change our brand and retell our stories.

By having a strong personal brand, regardless of whether we are branding for the first time, or we are rebranding ourselves, we are able to reap a great number of benefits. Firstly, we are able to gain a competitive advantage over other fellow professionals in the industry, especially those without a personal brand. We are also better able to stay relevant because our exercising of personal branding principles keeps us sharp and always aware of what's happening in the industry and market. We are also able to mitigate the negative effects of social media, which is ubiquitous in the digital age. Social media is what I

Introduction

describe as "the many watching the many". Accordingly, with a personal brand, we become more resilient to shocks in the market and industry. Finally, we will be able to send a clear signal to the market and industry as to what we stand for and what we have to offer.

But who do we know has a personal brand? All the successful politicians, entrepreneurs, businessmen and professionals whose names are familiar the world over have strong personal brands. Barack Obama, for one, has a strong personal brand. Everyone knows of his election as the first African-American president of the United States. His training and former career in civil rights law and academia served as the foundation for the skillset that he brought along with him into his political career. His values reflect his respect of liberty, equality and equity, and were clearly shown in his promotion of inclusivity. His tone of voice is always consistent and portrays a persona that is uniquely his. With this personal brand, no one can say, *Obama who?*

Jordan Belfort, the "Wolf of Wall Street", has a strong personal brand too. His innovation (albeit illegal) in seeing the value of penny stocks and how they could be a profitable business venture is well known all over the world. His ambition to succeed, as well as the generous rewards he gave to his top employees, was legendary and inspirational to scores of future entrepreneurs. Even today, Belfort still shares his professional opinions on matters concerning the business world, such as sales strategy, business ethics and cryptocurrency. Of course, having his character played by Leonardo DiCaprio helped immensely in cementing his name in popular culture.

Neil deGrasse Tyson has a strong personal brand. So does Oprah Winfrey. So does Patrick Bet-David. So does Zhang Weili. So does Batman.

What do all these big names have in common? Firstly, they all have a set of skills that are valued in the market and by the industry. They are respected for their professional views because they have mastered this set of skills that put them into a position of being "thought leaders". Secondly, they all have a persona that they carry around with them. They never step out of this persona (or go "off-brand") in any professional appearance they make. Thirdly, they always have a brand story. Their brand stories are the reason we look up to them. We know where they came from, where they are at the moment and where they are planning to be in the future. These are the three components of an effective personal brand.

It is important for you to understand how each of these components are laid out, so that you too can develop your own independent, conceptual frameworks as to how you would apply them to your own personal branding exercises. I will go into how we develop our brand persona starting with brand archetypes. I will also look at what *competencies* are, and how we can achieve mastery in our chosen competencies. Competencies are the foundations of our personal brands, while our brand persona is the "face" that we put forward. Finally, I will take a look at the principles of storytelling, and how we can put this method to good use in telling a story about our personal brands.

The world of business is not what it used to be. Times have changed and gotten more complex. Job roles have gotten more

Introduction

diverse. Gone are the days where a marketer only needed to do "above the line" advertising. These days, a digital marketer needs to know copywriting, content writing and some measure of graphic design, data analytics and UI/UX design too. Employment has become less and less permanent, and less and less certain. Gone are the days where employees were loyal to the company and companies took care of employees beyond retirement (when was the last time you heard of someone receiving a pension?). Gone are the days where people remained employed by the same company for decades on end. These days, professionals are not just employees. We are industry professionals who carry our weight through our personal brand and can contribute value to any company we choose to work with. Note, work *with*, not work *for*.

The business world today is powered by digitisation. Digitisation has not only changed our private lives through smartphones, smart homes and electronic payments. Digitisation has also seeped into the very fabric of our professional lives. Digitisation is ubiquitous and the world is just going to get more and more digital as we move from Web 2.0 to Web 3.0 (some people refer to this as simply web3). Digital diversity and digital density have increased since the early days of computing, and it's just going to get more diverse and more dense. Even digital platforms have risen and waned according to popular use. Yesterday it was MySpace, today it's TikTok, tomorrow all eyes are set on the Metaverse.

We as professionals cannot just respond to the changes in the business world. That is not sufficient. We must be in the eye of the tornado that is change. That is where we will be the safest. And how do we do that? Through personal branding.

We all need to understand that personal branding is not something that we only work on once in our lifetime. We need to maintain our personal brands by paying attention to the developments in the market and the industry. Even in the consumer market, brands don't always last forever. At one point in time, FUBU was the top name in urban clothing. At one point in time, Reebok was the top name in sports apparel. Today, there are other brands that have taken that mantle. Even in FMCG (fast-moving consumer goods), brands like Arm & Hammer and Frito-Lay have had to maintain their branding through paying close attention to the market in order to remain relevant. For us as professionals holding a personal brand, we need to continually respond to the market and industry. Should the changes be small, and don't affect our brand positioning in the market, we need to update ourselves. Should changes be small but do affect our brand positioning in the market, we might need to undergo a brand refresh. More major changes might call for a rebrand. In this instance, we also need to take action regarding what to do with our former personal brands when we rebrand. We have a choice as to whether we want to incorporate them into the brand we rebranded to, completely retire them, or keep them in hibernation until we can bring them back to life, perhaps in the future.

Introduction

The person, the professional, the personal brand

Personal branding is the process of creating a professional persona for ourselves with the requisite competencies (knowledge, skills and attitude) with a cohesive, comprehensible story, so as to continually retain our relevance as an industry professional. This personal brand should override any and all of our private inclinations, although in some instances there might be a permissible blurring of our private and professional selves.

Society places an archetype on professions, and this archetype is what they have come to expect of professionals in that profession. Should our private inclinations not fit that expectation, we must not allow our professional and private selves to share that same space in our personal brand. Otherwise, it might cause a fair bit of cognitive dissonance in how the industry and society perceive our professionalism. Take a look at the following scenario.

Jason is a corporate trainer. He spends his days training C-suite executives on optimising business processes and developing business opportunities. Jason speaks loudly, confidently and positively. He has a toolbox where he keeps all his templates for training, including business model canvases, customer journey maps and balanced scoresheets. At work, people continually compare him with Jordan Belfort, the Wolf of Wall Street. He seems to have that loud, confident air that always brings results. Yet, in private, Jason is an extreme introvert. Being around people tires him out. He prefers to spend his evenings in the comfort of his own home working on his bonsai and enjoying single malts from Islay. Do Jason's professional and private selves fit well with each other? Not to most people. As social animals, most people are quite partial to social life, and quite partial to extraversion. They expect others to love human company as much as they do. They also expect extroverts to be extroverts in both professional and private circumstances. Jason's preference for a quiet evening by himself sits uneasily in people's minds, thus, the cognitive dissonance. Cognitive dissonance is not a pleasant feeling to people in industry and society.

People in the industry and society often forget that individuals vary greatly between each other. They often forget that individuals vary greatly even within themselves. In fact, people are cognitively not quite able to acknowledge that. You see, humans cannot think of things existing in a continuum. Oh, they can see how colours blend, but the only way they can remember colours is to assign them names such as "red", "orange" and "yellow". These names are all subjective, judging by just how many variations of each colour (and accordingly, just as many names) there are. By extension, the only way most people can remember how a rainbow looks like is to assign it seven discrete colours: "red", "orange", "yellow", "green", "blue", "indigo" and "violet". But is a rainbow only made up of seven colours? No, of course not. There are a variety of colours as red blends into orange, as orange blends into yellow, as yellow blends into green, as green blends into blue, as blue blends into indigo and as indigo blends into violet. So why do we keep saying that rainbows have seven colours? Because that's the only way we can remember the colours of a rainbow.

Introduction

We apply this cognitive limitation of ours in every other aspect of life as well. We find it difficult to understand a person with a complex mixed parentage, unless the person offers specific categories to our understanding (for example, "I'm Scots-Irish on my dad's side and Chinese on my mom's side"). We find it difficult to understand another person's complex emotional state because to us, the feelings of happiness, sadness, disgust, fear, surprise, and anger are exhaustive and mutually exclusive. We find it difficult to understand why a person who is so bubbly and outgoing at his job would prefer to have a contemplative, quiet evening alone.

So what should Jason do? Jason should craft a personal brand to be seen by the public that promotes his professional self. Jason should not allow his private self to be seen by the public, at least not without dressing it up a little to match it with his professional self.

But isn't that being "fake"? Shouldn't we just "be ourselves". No. A big flat no. As I said, individuals vary greatly between and within themselves. Not every bit of us is palatable to every single person in society. In fact, sociologist Erving Goffman wrote at length about "front stage" and "back stage" in personal behaviours. Every single one of us has consciously, unconsciously or subconsciously behaved in such a way that we present our best selves when we know that we are interfacing with others. We know that there are certain behaviours that are best kept private (such as farting, picking our noses or talking to ourselves). We learn all this from the process of socialisation, where we learn about behaviours and social expectations as we grow up.

This is because we've grown up learning that there are some behaviours and thoughts that are best kept private because not everyone will agree with how we think, how we act and what we choose to do. Some of us have furkids. We love our furkids to bits. We pamper our furkids so much that we don't see them as being of a different species from us. We're not too keen on having human children though, as nice as they may seem. We love furkids too much. Yet, this does not sit well with everyone. Why, even the Pope made a statement that people who choose to have furkids over human children are being "selfish". And if having furkids doesn't sit too well with the Pope, you know it's not going to sit well with many other Roman Catholics too. (The Popes were influencers way before Instagram was even incorporated.)

As the French sociologist Emile Durkheim said, "In a society of saints there will still be sinners." What this means is that the objectionability of our private inclinations is almost entirely dependent on societal norms. If we live in a highly conservative society, or work in a highly conservative industry or organisation, even the slightest deviation from the norm will be looked upon objectionably. "Oh, I see you put coriander on your pizza. How strange. Shouldn't you be sprinkling oregano instead? The rest of us do. I guess you must be special. Or on a slippery slope to a life of deviance."

And on the flip side, not all of us agree with the predominant norms, values, attitudes and practices in society too. As delicious as it may be, not all of us enjoy apple pie. We as individuals accordingly react to society as well. Many of us may already have a cognitive predisposition to apple pie. We enjoy it as much as the next guy. We don't understand how anyone could not like it. Others may convince themselves that apple pie is the way to go. We construct this idea that if others like it, so should we. Yet others may just act like we like apple pie. We say "yum" and rub our tums with glee with every bite but no, we don't really like it. And yet others may rebel against this entire dessert and fight for our rights to enjoy the pie of our own choosing.

Our personal brands must complement apple pie, that dessert that everyone in society has come to expect as the baseline dessert. Some of our personal brands already complement apple pie. Great. Some of our personal brands may need to be constructed in such a way that they seem complementary to apple pie. Some of our personal brands may need to act as a good complement to apple pie. But to go against apple pie totally is not a good idea. Always remember that the success of our personal branding depends largely on the receiving public. Industry and society must acknowledge our personal brand in order for our personal brand to be accepted, validated and legitimised.

The roadmap

Whenever I educate, consult or mentor, I always like to provide both a "whole-to-part" structure as well as a "step-by-step" structure to the information I present. This is because in all my years of experience, I have discovered that some of us prefer to learn via a "whole-to-part" sequencing, while others prefer to learn via a "step-by-step" sequencing. A "whole-to-part" sequencing is where information is presented in the "bigger picture" first, followed by the parts that make up that bigger picture. Some of us prefer this sequencing because we want to customise the learning materials for our specific needs. We want to think critically, and be creative in application. We try to see how each specific part fits in, and want to decide for ourselves which parts are more relevant to us than others. This "whole-to-part" sequencing shall be provided in Chapters 2 through 4. In Chapter 2, I shall give the bigger picture of personal branding and then break it down into its three component parts, namely, the brand persona, competencies and storytelling. I shall break down each component part even further into their sub-parts. Under the brand persona, I shall look at "brand archetypes" and how they form the basis of the development of a brand persona. I shall look at how archetypes can be amalgamated into a brand personality. I then will look at the components of a brand persona that should be developed, including the brand voice, brand values (and anti-values) and brand visual identity. Under "competencies", I shall touch on the three components of competencies, namely, knowledge, skills and attitude. These are primarily descriptive components, but what would be more helpful are the components of developing competency. In this regard, I shall touch on "learning", "practising" and "applying". Learning is where we pick up the knowledge. Practising is where we develop the skills. Applying is where we begin our road to mastery. Do note though that there isn't just one level of mastery. We could master our chosen competencies like a master, or a master among masters. In other words, we could be a rec centre karate coach, or we could be Bruce Lee. Finally, I shall

Introduction

delve into the sub-parts of storytelling as well. I will look into the method of storytelling, which is a method developed for presenting facts and information in a memorable, easy-to-consume manner. This method was developed from our observations of various stories (such as folk tales, Bible stories, movies and such) and the effect these stories had on us. As part of this method, I will look at how to structure our personal brand stories using story plots, and how to spice up our stories using Ancient Greek modes of persuasion. The whole, its component parts and the sub-parts of each component are presented to you so that you may exercise your wilful judgement in deciding which part speaks to you more. Which part has been missing from your life thus far? Which part gave you a "wow" moment? Which part should you prioritise in your own personal branding exercise? Which part can you afford to give a miss?

But wait, there's more. I don't just stop at giving you a theoretical and conceptual insight into brand personas, competencies and storytelling. I extend the "whole-to-part" configuration by looking at the rationale behind personal branding in Chapter 3. I will expound upon the benefits one can have with a personal brand. I will go into how having a personal brand can help a professional gain competitive advantage in the market vis-a-vis other professionals, especially those without a personal brand. I will also look at how having a personal brand will urge professionals to stay relevant in the market and industry, as they will be attuned to keeping an eye on developments which require their attention and action. At the expense of dampening the mood, I will also look at a particular cultural characteristic of today's digital world, which is where everyone is watching and judging each other through social media ("the many watching the many"). Having a personal brand, and being aware of how the many watching the many can have an adverse effect on our personal brands will bring awareness to us as professionals as to how we should stay within our brand limits. I also look at how a professional with a personal brand is also equipped to withstand shocks in the market and industry. This gives him greater resilience than those who do not have personal brands. Finally, I will also look at how having a personal brand gives a clear signal to the market industry. This helps us greatly in matching our brand persona with the specific requirements of employers, clients and collaborators. This is important because different employers, clients and collaborators have different requirements in terms of competencies they require to support them and the types of personality they wish to work with. In this regard, I urge you to think of potential employers, clients and collaborators as your "target market". Some of them will be your primary target market, while others will be your secondary and tertiary target markets.

    I further extend the "whole-to-part" configuration by looking at the temporal considerations for personal branding in Chapter 4. I urge you to begin your personal branding exercise as soon as you can. I will also look at some conditions which would require you to refresh your brand, especially those conditions which may put you slightly out of sync with what the market needs. I will also look at some more pressing conditions which would require you to rebrand. Upon rebranding, I will

Introduction

lay out three ways in which you could decide on what to do with your former personal brand. You may choose to incorporate it into your new brand, or retire it completely, or keep it in hibernation until such a time when you can thaw it out and reuse it again. Conceptually, I will rely on the concept of "house of brands", where you, the professional, are the "house of brands" that can hold many brands at the same time. It is your decision which brand to promote as your flagship brand, and which brand to relegate to a side brand.

Now, as I mentioned, there are others who prefer a more "step-by-step" sequencing to learning. They prefer a more step-by-step approach because they are cautious about which steps to take. They prefer to work with an established template, rather than try having a go at it on their own. But that's okay too. I will go into a step-by-step set of recommendations in Chapters 5 to 8. In Chapter 5, I will look into how you should first develop competencies as the foundation of your personal brand. Competencies should precede everything else in personal branding. In modern, industrial, capitalist societies, our value lies in what we can bring to the table. As professionals, what we can bring to the table are the competencies we possess. I will go through each step in detail, using some important frameworks borrowed from business studies, user experience research and instructional design. In Chapter 6, I will look into how you can develop your own brand persona. Look, Stephen Hawking was not just another astrophysicist. There are plenty of astrophysicists around, but we remember Stephen Hawking. Freddie Mercury was not just another singer. There are plenty of other singers around, some better, some worse, some as good as Freddie. But we remember him fondly. What is it about such people that makes them stand out? It's their brand personas. In developing your own brand persona, I will provide you here with tabular guides that hopefully simplify the process for you. In Chapter 7, I look at storytelling. I will show how you can package your competencies and brand personas in your brand stories so that your brand can be more memorable and engaging, making it all the more effective. Again, I will give step-by-step recommendations on how to structure and spice up your brand story.

Chapter 8 is a bonus. It is about optimising your personal brand. By "optimising", what I mean is how to maximise its effectiveness. I will look at how you can keep your eye on the market and industry in order to continually keep your brand fresh and relevant. I will also look at how you can update your digital presence, which is increasingly important in this digital era. Gone are the days where our reputation was spread through "word of mouth". Gone are the days where we exchanged name cards and shook hands over wine and cheese at networking sessions. These days, our digital presence determines our visibility. I will also look at how you can watch out for threats. Just like in some other chapters, I will borrow some concepts from risk management here to highlight to you the kind of threats that we face as professionals. I will break down the threats that we should watch out most for, and how to mitigate them.

It is hoped that with everything that I provide you with here, you will consider developing your personal brand. There can be no overcrowding in a space filled with personal brands.

Introduction

There can be no "red ocean" where every personal brand is competing with other personal brands to win contracts, get jobs or secure collaborations. In fact, it is just the opposite. Personal branding helps you break out of these tight and crowded market situations because there are an infinite number of permutations of personal brands. Margaret Cho is an Asian-American comedian. So is Ali Wong. So is Awkwafina. Do we mistake them for each other? Did the comedy space somehow get smaller with one extra entrant into the comedy market? No. The space remains the same, because each one of these comedians has their own unique personal brand.

CHAPTER 2

The Conceptual Grounding of Personal Branding

A personal brand is a cohesive, comprehensive set of symbols, skills and story that can be used to represent and define an industry professional. It is composed of the professional's brand persona, competencies and brand story that the professional carries around. A personal brand must appear complete but the personal branding exercise is never completed. It is always both constant and in flux at the same time. A personal brand makes the difference between someone who is merely an employee of an organisation, and an industry professional.

But what really is an industry professional? An industry professional is a professional who is always relevant and active in the industry that he is in. He is not just an employee of an organisation. He can be of help to any organisation in the industry because he has mastery of his domain. He's not begging for a job from any organisation. He's saying to potential employers, clients and collaborators, "Look, I've got these skills and experience. I can help you. If you'd like me to help you, I'll be happy to. I'd like to see if you can help me too". An industry professional works *with*, not *for*, another person.

For an industry professional, a persona helps us put an image, or a face, to our professional selves. This component is important in helping us "talk the talk". Competencies, on the other hand, allow us to "walk the walk". We can't just have a persona without any competencies. We would just be an empty vessel. We wouldn't be able to perform as an industry professional without any relevant or requisite competencies. Competencies, in turn, comprise knowledge, skills and attitude. It is not sufficient to have the knowledge. We must be able to turn that knowledge into action through skills. And we must also have a holistic attitude towards the area of competency, looking at the subject matter from all angles and all perspectives. We cannot adopt a transactional attitude (where one can only follow direct instruction) towards the subject matter.

Telling our brand story is important for making our brand heard. Without telling the story, there is no way we can build brand awareness. Our terminal objective should be to build top-of-mind brand recall, where people in the industry immediately think about our personal brand whenever any topic related to our areas of expertise is mentioned. The character of Akeem, played by Eddie Murphy in *Coming to America*, alluded to top-of-mind brand recall when he said, "When you think of garbage, think of Akeem." Beyond that, you should also think about building brand advocacy, where people in the industry recommend your brand to others. Whether it be through the traditional "word of mouth" spread or through leaving good reviews about you on LinkedIn, or through tagging you in social media posts, brand advocacy is very helpful in keeping current customers coming back for repeat engagements and getting new customers without spending extra time, effort and money. By keeping current customers coming back for repeat engagements, we are increasing each customer's "customer lifetime value". By spending less time, effort and money acquiring new customers, we are lowering our "customer acquisition cost". A high customer lifetime value and a low customer acquisition cost are the most tangible benefits of having a strong personal brand. More on the benefits of personal branding in Chapter 3. First, let's take a look at the theoretical and conceptual foundations of brand persona, competencies and storytelling, shall we?

Brand persona

Whenever I engage in branding exercises for companies, the first thing I do is to lay out brand archetypes. Brand archetypes are directly derived from Swiss psychoanalyst Carl Jung's 12 human archetypes (as mentioned in *On the Nature of the Psyche* (1954) and *The Archetypes and the Collective Unconscious* (1969)). These 12 archetypes have in turn been derived from the characters that we have been accustomed to encountering in the stories we've seen, read, watched and heard.

Of course, a disclaimer should be given here. These 12 archetypes are a Western interpretation of a set of Western stories whose characters were created using Western ideas. They are by no means universal across all cultures. If we were to look deeply at the stories from other cultures, we will be able to find different archetypes that are more suited to that culture. The Chinese classic, *Journey to the West*, has different archetypes, and so does the African import into America, Brer Rabbit. However, for the purposes of simplicity of analysis and a way forward for this book, I shall be using Jung's archetypes as a framework for our analysis (members of the "woke" generation, please don't "cancel" Jung!).

The 12 archetypes are:

1. Outlaw: A combative, rebellious character who lives on the fringes of societal acceptance
2. Magician: A character shrouded in mystery who can perform miracles through fantasy and illusion
3. Hero: A brave, larger-than-life character who protects and defends
4. Lover: A sensual character that connects to our more basal, intimate human aspects
5. Jester: A playful, happy-go-lucky character that is full of humour and doesn't take life too seriously
6. Everyman: A character who is an all-round nice guy and is happy to be amongst the salt of the earth

7. Caregiver: A caring, warm character who comforts those around him
8. Ruler: A commanding, authoritative character who takes control of his life and environment
9. Creator: A character who is innovative, known for his fresh ideas and inventive capacities
10. Innocent: A slightly naive, honest character who has a child-like appeal
11. Sage: An informed, wise character who guides and advises others
12. Explorer: A fearless, daring character who is not afraid of trying something new and going into uncharted territory

As I said, I always begin any company branding exercise by laying out these 12 archetypes. Upon laying out these archetypes, I make the stakeholders agree on two things. Firstly, they must agree that they are not going to make any mention of the pricing of their products. They must agree that they are not going to use price as a unique value proposition. Why? Because making mention of price would inevitably lead them into a price war with their competitors. They would need to either match their competitor's prices or go lower in order to win a share of the market, without accounting for the quality of their products, or the cost of producing their products. A price war would subject their products to price elasticity. Customers would be inclined to buy from the company that sells at the lower price. In a price war, a branding exercise would be completely unnecessary.

But, with a strong brand, on the other hand, price would not matter. The company's products will be price inelastic. That is to say, their customers would buy from them regardless of the price they charge. Why is that? Because a company with a strong brand would develop its products specifically according to its unique brand persona, which matches the personalities of its target market. And because of that, the target market will in turn see the products as being specific to their wants and needs and thus not easily substitutable for products by other companies. If you were a fan of Armani Exchange, for example, would you just as easily switch over to Giordano just because the latter is cheaper? Why not? Both are streetwear, aren't they? The reason is because you see a close affinity between your own personality and the persona that Armani Exchange exudes. You don't see an affinity between yourself and Giordano, and hence, you won't be easily swayed to substitute one for the other.

Secondly, they must agree that in order for branding to proceed, the company must be personified. That is to say, companies must be seen as a person, as a human being. It is important to imagine companies as a person because only by doing so can we think about how to align companies' branding strategies with their target market. At the most basic level, companies have a vision, a mission and values. Potential customers have wants and needs. Customers would want to satisfy their wants and needs with a company that upholds the same values as they do. They would want to satisfy their wants and needs with a company that has a vision that they respect. They would want to satisfy their wants and needs with a company that is on a mission that they identify with. If the company is a person, its target customers may then be thought of as the company's "friends". As a corollary, birds of a feather would flock together.

Once we've got these two conditions out of the way, I will then get the companies under the branding exercises to choose archetype(s) for themselves. A company that chooses to personify itself as an Outlaw, such as Harley Davidson, would work towards creating a persona of itself in that archetype. Consequently, a set of potential customers who see themselves similarly as outlaws would be attracted to that image, and become drawn to that brand (the potential customers don't need to be actual criminals, they just need to have an image of themselves as "outlaws", kind of like how chihuahuas think of themselves as being more fearsome than pitbulls). The same goes for brands that choose to personify themselves as any of the other 11 archetypes. Empathetic individuals would be more attracted to Caregiver brands, sensual, amorous individuals would be more attracted to Lover brands, and so on.

It is important to note that most companies do not just choose one archetype. They must choose at least two, in order to be able to successfully brand themselves. Why is that? Well, they firstly would choose one *core* archetype that represents themselves as well as every other similar company that provides similar products and services. Thus, the Creator archetype is most often used by technology companies because of its proclivity to innovation and invention, just as the Caregiver archetype is most often used by healthcare companies because of its emphasis on healing and wellness. The Lover archetype is most often

The Conceptual Grounding of Personal Branding

used by lingerie companies because of its emphasis on sensuousness and intimacy.

And then, to differentiate themselves from one another, companies would then choose an *influencer* archetype, which appeals directly to the collective personalities of their intended target market. The core and influencer archetypes would be amalgamated together to form a new personality. A total of 132 personalities can result from the various combinations of two archetypes alone. Some companies might choose more than two influencer archetypes, giving them even more possibilities in branding.

Archetype	Core Personality	Amalgamator	Influencer Personality
Outlaw	Combative and rebellious		Combative and rebellious
Magician	Mysterious and miraculous		Mysterious and miraculous
Hero	Strong and protective		Strong and protective
Lover	Sensual and intimate		Sensual and intimate
Jester	Playful and happy-go-lucky		Playful and happy-go-lucky
Everyman	Easy-going and pleasant	But is also	Easy-going and pleasant
Caregiver	Caring and empathetic		Caring and empathetic
Ruler	Commanding and authoritative		Commanding and authoritative
Creator	Innovative and inventive		Innovative and inventive
Innocent	Naive and honest		Naive and honest
Sage	Wise and guiding		Wise and guiding
Explorer	Intrepid and experimental		Intrepid and experimental

Rebrand Yourself, Retell Your Story

The resultant persona could be, for example, the core archetype of an Explorer with an influencer archetype of a Jester. In combination, this personification would be an intrepid traveller who always sees the bright side of life. The low-cost carrier SuperAirJet is an example of this combination of archetypes. As an airline, it bases itself on the core archetype of an Explorer because travellers often look for new experiences on their travels. The Jester archetype comes in because it designs its branding to be specifically for the "millennial experience". It tries to meet the wants and needs of millennial travellers, and even sports uniforms that are less formal and more casual. This can be seen in contrast to another low-cost carrier, AirAsia, which is a combination of Explorer and Everyman. The founder of AirAsia structured the airline's pricing model as an affordable way to travel for the average Joe. And its branding followed suit.

Following the amalgamation of its core and influencer archetypes, the company would then create a persona (or brand image) of itself. The company must ensure that all the components of their persona, as shown below, gel well with each other:

- Brand name: A name that is suitable and appropriate for the persona created
- Brand slogan: A sentence or phrase that could cognitively be associated with that persona
- Brand voice: The tone of voice, composed of chosen lexicon and grammar, that would appear on the brand's social media and other advertisements

The Conceptual Grounding of Personal Branding

- Brand values: What the brand stands for
- Brand anti-values: What the brand is against
- Brand visual identity: The brand's logo, corporate colours and guidelines for photography, videography, graphics and illustrations
- Brand vision: The ambition of the brand
- Brand mission: The activities of the brand in order to realise that ambition

Here is an example of a persona that is comprehensive across its components. This kind of persona construction would result in a strong brand. The dark theme of the brand flows across all components of the persona and would thus come through effectively to the target market. Similarly dark individuals would receive this message loud and clear, and consequently find this brand attractive. (Yes, there are such persons around, as hard as it is to believe. No, they're not clinically depressed, they just have a different perspective on life.)

- Brand name: Coal Hard Heart
- Brand slogan: Colour me black
- Brand voice: Should always use words which are connotative of dreariness. Err on the side of melancholy and dark melodrama.
- Brand values: Darkness, despair, fatalism and nihilism
- Brand anti-values: Positivity and optimism
- Brand visual identity: The brand's logo should use gunmetal grey as its primarily colour, with accents of blood

red and white. The shape should feature acute angles with organic shapes. The logo, photographs and illustrations should take inspiration from the "biomechanical" and "post-apocalyptic" art styles.
- Brand vision: To be the market leader in clothing and accessories that reflect feelings of a constant melancholic state of heart and mind.
- Brand mission: Creating products that would appeal to the darkest of hearts so that what they feel on the inside can be reflective on what they wear on the outside.

We can clearly see what the brand stands for. It's a fashion brand for people who have a dark perspective on life. It's definitely going to attract people from the goth and metal subcultures, people who are fans of Nietzsche's writing, and people who are fans of dark-themed art (such as "grotesque art", "dark deco" and "pop surrealism"). I see this brand in a similar vein to Alchemy England and Clocks and Colours.

In contrast, here is an example of a persona that is not consistent across its components. Why is it not consistent? Some parts of the persona suggest warmth, happiness and sunshine, while other parts of the persona suggest dirt, grit and grime. It would be like if SpongeBob SquarePants donned Batman's suit and tried to fight crime. Does that brand persona work for you? As a joke, maybe. As a novelty, maybe. Not as a brand to continually identify with. Why? Because it is confusing. This kind of persona construction would not result in a strong brand.

The Conceptual Grounding of Personal Branding

- Brand name: Swansong
- Brand slogan: The bigger they are, the harder they fall.
- Brand voice: Should always use words which are connotative of happiness. Err on the side of naivete and warmth.
- Brand values: Positivity and optimism.
- Brand anti-values: None, because positive people are never anti anything
- Brand visual identity: The brand's logo should use baby pink as its primarily colour, with accents of baby blue and neon green. The shape should feature obtuse angles with geometric shapes. The logo, photographs and illustrations should take inspiration from the "cubism" and "vaporwave" art styles.
- Brand vision: To be the market leader in clothing and accessories that reflect feelings of a happy child.
- Brand mission: Creating products that would appeal to a more industrial look but suitable for daily street fashion.

First off, the brand name Swansong is double-edged. While a swan is beautiful and a song is a pleasant sonic expression, "swansong" gives a melancholic sense of finality. It is the final gift before someone retires or passes away. Not a good image to start off with. The brand slogan does not make sense. Why is there a reference to size and combat? Are they selling self-defence equipment? Well, at least the brand personality makes sense, right? Not until you see the brand voice and brand values.

How can anyone so gritty and grimy be so happy? The brand visual identity is equally confusing. The palette is unsuitable, and the art references cannot be any more awkward. The brand vision and the brand mission also are very strange bedfellows. Happy children do not wear industrial clothing. Have you seen a toddler playing with fallen leaves dressed as the characters from Mad Max?

It is important for companies to constantly remind themselves that the brand is not the business, and the business is not the brand. The business side of the company is concerned with revenue, cost and solvency. The branding side of the company is concerned with imagery. The brand is the public "face", while the business is the beating heart and working brain. Business modelling is a separate exercise from branding and when I conduct a business modelling exercise, I would focus on value propositions, partners, resources, activities, customer relationships, sales, supply and distribution channels, customer segmentation, cost structures and revenue streams.

So where do the brand and the business meet? A strong brand acts as a magnet to attract potential customers. And these customers would be the ones whose dollars would sustain the business. Just as Kelis sings, "My milkshake brings all the boys to the yard." A strong brand enables the business to benefit from having a lower customer acquisition cost and a higher customer lifetime value. The brand and the business are two sides of a company that are intricately linked, but work separately from each other.

Can a brand exist without the business side? Oh, sure. If

money is not a concern, of course a brand can exist without the business side. Non-profit organisations fit that model very well. Some influencers on social media who don't have anything to sell and don't do any paid/branded promotions but nonetheless have tons of followers fit this model too.

Can a business exist without a brand? Oh, sure. Businesses that are in perfect competition with each other, such as two ice-cream sellers along a beach selling the same flavours of ice-cream, are businesses without a brand. Most fast-moving consumer goods (FMCG) sellers on online marketplaces are also businesses without a brand. They primarily engage in a price war with each other, and are only interested in revenue. Without a brand, they are unable to obtain a high customer lifetime value and a lower customer acquisition cost. Customers will only buy from the seller who offers the best monetary value, such as the cheapest price or the quickest delivery.

It is also important for companies to acknowledge that the branding exercise is not terminal. Brands must constantly monitor and maintain their brand reputation in order to continue to be relevant to the market. Companies may need to engage in a "brand refresh" exercise sometime in the future so as to update themselves with the changing trends, especially among their target market. When the business environment changes more drastically, though, brands may need to rebrand. Rebranding is when companies redo the branding process by rethinking their personas and their intended target markets. A brand such as Dr. Martens, for example, is famous for having rebranded from a Caregiver archetype to an Outlaw archetype. In its initial conception, it produced shoes for middle-aged ladies with podiatric issues. It later rebranded itself as an Outlaw when the punk subculture took to their shoes (as well as the shoes of its former partner, Solovair) as a mainstay of punk fashion. This new branding is clearly evident in its product design, social media, advertisements and public events.

Personal brand persona

All these ideas and methods for company branding can be applied to personal branding for professionals too. Do note that here in this section, I will only be sharing a general application of branding methods to personal branding. This is not (yet) the step-by-step process, which will only come in Chapters 5 through 8.

Now, just as I made companies undergoing a branding exercise agree on the pre-conditions of branding, I will also make professionals undergoing a personal branding exercise agree on pre-conditions.

Firstly, you must agree that you cannot and must not see yourself as primarily an employee of an organisation. Seeing yourself as primarily an employee is disadvantageous because you tend to get lulled by the comforts of the company and pay less attention to the developments in the larger market and industry. As a result, you might not see the need to gain a competitive advantage against other fellow professionals in the industry. Gaining a competitive advantage is very important if you wish to "cut through the mix" and get noticed as a professional. Furthermore, if you get lulled by the comforts of the company, you might not be motivated to stay relevant to the industry. Sure, you would definitely want to stay relevant in the company, but do remember that whatever your company sees as a prerogative may be different from what the industry sees as a prerogative. Your company may ask you to wear different hats or pick up different skills because it makes sense to them. But it may not make sense to the larger industry. What you do for the company may not be what the industry actually needs. Thirdly, if you get lulled by the comforts of the company, you may lose resilience. I understand that your company may promise to protect you at all costs, but I do advise you to build your own resilience as well. Think of it as private insurance. Or a prenuptial agreement. It doesn't hurt to build that extra layer of protection.

Secondly, you must agree to separate the professional from the private. Look, we all have private personalities. Personalities are something that even science cannot explain. Twins brought up the same way in the same household may develop different personalities as they grow up. Personality development is highly dependent on how we perceive incoming sensory stimuli, how we incorporate them into our existing schemas (the body of knowledge that we store in our minds) and how we learn from experiences. While one twin may perceive a reward for doing well in school as positive reinforcement and recognition of effort, the other twin might perceive it as an act of condescension. While one twin may perceive a reprimand for truancy as a wake-up call, the other twin may perceive it as a challenge to be better at playing truant. There is nothing wrong with our private personalities. We are at liberty to be who we are. However, the industry and the market have expectations of how certain professionals should think and act. And a lot of the time, our private personalities do not exactly fit the expectations of our professions. The risk we want to mitigate with this agreement is the risk of having our private lives adversely affect our professional lives.

Now that I have your agreement, we can begin. Earlier I mentioned how I get companies to personify themselves in order to choose brand archetypes. It is important for companies to see the human element in themselves so that they can create a relationship, a friendship if you will, with members of their intended target market.

To apply these principles to personal branding, we will use the "deeper reaper" method. This is an abbreviation for "depersonification-repersonification" (but you can also think of it as the deeper you go into personal branding, the more benefits you will reap). As the name suggests, the first step in this method is to depersonify ourselves. It may seem counterintuitive but in order for us to build a personal brand, we would need to depersonify ourselves first. Why? Because we need to separate the professional from the private. By depersonifying ourselves, we are thus able to see that our professional selves need not be the same as our private personalities. We are thus able to think of ourselves as a completely different person from who we know ourselves to be. It allows us to start on a blank slate and develop our personal brands based on our professional selves.

The next step in the "deeper reaper" method is to repersonify by choosing a core archetype. This is based on the industry

The Conceptual Grounding of Personal Branding

or the job role that you are in. Comedians, emcees and other entertainers would easily find themselves aligning with the Jester archetype. Tech entrepreneurs, devops engineers and "makers" (semi-professionals who tinker with tech hardware) would easily find themselves aligning with the Creator archetype. Teachers, professors and business consultants would easily find themselves aligning with the Sage archetype.

    As for choosing an influencer archetype, this is not as crucial to personal branding as it is to company branding. It is quite sufficient to just stop at the core archetype if we wish to sport the same image as others in the same industry or job role. At times, it could be the safe thing to do as well, especially if we belong to industries, organisations or cultures that demand conformity. In Japan, for example, they say that "the nail that sticks out is hammered down". In such contexts, all nurses should be seen as Caregivers and nothing more. All military personnel should be seen as Heroes and nothing more. All C-suite executives should be seen as Rulers and nothing more.

    However, if we wish, are willing and are able to distinguish ourselves from others in the same profession or industry, we would then proceed to choose an influencer archetype. By doing so, we are able to create a closer relationship with others in the industry (such as employers, clients or collaborators) who are also of that same archetype. This closer relationship can do wonders for building trust in our personal brand, and to promote top-of-mind recall of our personal brand. In other words, we have a chance at being the "go to" brand of choice in the industry rather than just one among the many. Many of the colourful characters that we come across in popular media feature a core archetype and at least one influencer archetype. Dr Cox's personal brand in *Scrubs* is a Caregiver at his core (as a surgeon) but is also a Ruler (a disciplinarian to his subordinates) and a Magician (someone who is able to perform difficult surgeries) as his influencer archetypes. Gomer Pyle is a Hero at his core (as a soldier) but is also a Jester (happy-go-lucky) and an Everyman (your average guy next door). The resultant brand personality would thus contain adjectives to describe their professional persona. Just as it is for company branding, the brand personality for professionals would be derived from the amalgamation of their core and influencer archetypes. For example, an educational technologist (someone who works with e-learning platforms and learning management systems) who has appropriately chosen the Sage (the "ed" part of his brand) and the Creator (the "tech" part of his brand) would thus be "wise" and "innovative".

And as it is for companies, personal brands too need a comprehensive, consistent and coherent persona. In the case of personal brands, professionals could craft the following components, as appropriate to their chosen archetypes:

- Brand name: What do they want to call themselves? Many professionals come up with creative names for themselves these days. I have seen a CEO call himself "Company Yakuza". I've seen a business consultant call herself a "Catalyst for Change". I've seen a cybersecurity specialist call himself a "Monochrome Hat Hacker".

The Conceptual Grounding of Personal Branding

- Brand slogan: A saying that they would often use as a professional. Practitioners of "Management 3.0" are often fond of saying "Manage the system, not the people". Similarly, the motto of National Technical Investigators Association, "In God we trust, all others we monitor", has been used by many project managers whose key responsibilities include project monitoring and milestone reporting.
- Brand voice: The tone of voice, composed of chosen lexicon and grammar, that would appear on the professional's social media, website and other interactions. In other words, what words would the professional use? Technical jargon? Simpler synonyms that have a more casual connotation? Synonyms which have a more formal connotation? What grammar would he use? Syntax that is closer to written language? Syntax that is closer to corporate language? Syntax that is closer to regional or dialect use?
- Brand values: What the professional stands for. These show the things that he believes in. For example, a veterinarian could strongly believe that all creatures are created equal. A lawyer could believe that justice will always prevail. Brand values could be optimistic, pragmatic, realistic or sometimes even nihilistic. I've encountered an educator whose brand values are all about positivity and opportunity. I've encountered risk managers whose brand values are all about managing risk at the expense of opportunities. Why, I've

even encountered a career coach whose brand values are all about fearing the imminent takeover of technology (and artificial intelligence, in particular). For personal brands, these values would speak the loudest to the audience. Employers, clients and collaborators who share the same values as the professional are most likely to align themselves with the professional.

- Brand anti-values: What the professional is against. Values and anti-values stand at opposites to each other. The brand values define the personal brand perimeter, while the anti-values define the area outside of permissible personal brand limits. Should the professional step into the anti-values territory, he would be going off-brand. A financial advisor could believe in creating legitimate wealth for his clients (values) and on the opposite side, is against unethical financial practices (anti-values). Should he conduct unethical financial practices himself, he would be going off-brand. The employers, clients and collaborators who aligned with him would lose trust in him.
- Brand visual identity: The professional should think for himself how he should appear to the public. If he were to be an Everyman, should he be wearing clothes that someone of median income cannot afford? If he were to be a Sage, should he allow himself to appear in video interviews as unprepared and ignorant? The more astute professionals would go further to create for themselves a personal brand logo, accompanied by

The Conceptual Grounding of Personal Branding

corporate colours suitable to the chosen archetypes.
- Brand vision: The ambition of the professional. Where does he see himself going in the long run? What does he want to be? Tech startup founders and social enterprise founders know the importance of vision very well. Many tech startup founders see themselves and their companies as "unicorns". Unicorns want to disrupt the current market with a special, unique product offering. They want to experience exponential growth and eventually conquer the market by acquiring all the users from an existing technological product. Many social enterprise founders see themselves and their companies as "zebras". Zebras prioritise "purpose before profits". They see themselves making a change in the world to groups in society that they feel for, such as animals, disabled persons or elderly persons. They believe strongly in sustainable prosperity.
- Brand mission: The activities of the professional in order to realise that ambition. That is to say, what would the professionals do in order to reach the vision for themselves? Would they be founding a company? Would they be offering pro bono services? Would they mentor others?

As you can see, the creation of a persona for a professional brand is not very different from personifying a company for branding. More importantly, the creation of a persona is one of the three important components of a personal brand. The other two important components, as defined earlier, are competencies and storytelling. We will get to them in the next section.

Here is an example of a good personal brand persona. It is aligned across its components, and gives a clear message of what the professional is about.

- Real name: Jensen Doe
- Profession: Operations Manager
- Brand personality: Systematic, logical, rational, cautiously optimistic
- Brand name: Business Systems Optimiser
- Brand slogan: Trust the process
- Brand voice: Should always use words which do not have strong connotations or innuendo. Err on the side of formality.
- Brand values: Cautious optimism, problem-solving, constant testing and iteration.
- Brand anti-values: Constant firefighting, perennial stop-gap measures.
- Brand visual identity: The brand's logo should use traffic light green and traffic light amber as its two primary colours with accents of black. The shape should feature obtuse angles with geometric shapes. The logo, photographs and illustrations should take inspiration from the "polygonal" and "art deco" art styles.
- Brand vision: To lead by way of systemic thought, systemic operations and systemic interactions.
- Brand mission: Implementing systems that

create seamless human-computer interactions in organisations.

We can see that Jensen is a professional specialising in business systems. He sees the value of people and technology, and wishes for them to communicate more effectively. After all, he knows that some people are technophobic. And many enterprise systems cannot integrate well with each other. Just like the systems he heralds, Jensen exhibits systemic thought and systemic behaviour too. Now, if I were to be a potential employer, client or collaborator, I would look to Jensen if I, too, saw the importance of systems in organisations. I would be attracted to his personal brand because it lauds the same values as I do. However, if I place greater emphasis on other matters aside from management by systems, I would not look to Jensen. Some companies, for example, are more concerned with sales turnover. Companies like these place a huge emphasis on sales, of course. They are not too concerned about their processes, as long as the end objective (sales) is met. Having a strong personal brand like this is also helpful to Jensen. Would he want to work with a company that places more emphasis on sales rather than operations? Of course not. He would be dissatisfied with the direction and emphasis of the company.

Now, here is an example of a poor personal brand persona. It is misaligned across its components, and does not give a clear message of what the professional is about. It contains too many ambiguities that do not make for a recognisable and memorable persona. It is also confusing because some components of the persona don't fit well with the others. Furthermore, many components of the persona look outdated and not suitable to the current era.

- Real name: Joaquin Doe
- Profession: Career coach
- Brand personality: Creative, critical, analytical
- Brand name: Positive psychologist
- Brand slogan: Automation will take your job away
- Brand voice: Should always use words which are connotative of morality and mortality.
- Brand values: Hard work, honesty, punctuality
- Brand anti-values: Laziness, job-hopping
- Brand visual identity: The brand's logo should use gold and royal purple. The shapes should feature organic curves and a leafy motif. The logo, photographs and illustrations should take inspiration from the "cyber" and "military chic" art styles.
- Brand vision: To fit young people into their first job as expediently as possible.
- Brand mission: Creating value for the economy by supplying hardworking labour.

What is Joaquin's brand about? I know that positive psychology is helpful in career coaching, but does everyone else know that? It is too vague to make sense to the market and industry. Why would he warn against automation? Isn't automation inevitable and going to be ever more entrenched as we step deeper into the digital era? With artificial intelligence and more Web 3.0 builds, automation is not going away. And why is his brand voice defined by morality and mortality? Is he a career coach or an undertaker? Plus, take a look at his brand values and anti-values. When was the last time you heard the term "job-hopping"? Joaquin wants to party like it's 1989 it seems. The brand visual identity of leafy motifs, gold and royal purple also does not fit in with the rest. It's just too regal and aloof for a career coach. Couple that with the art styles mentioned. I guess Joaquin is trying to be a dictatorial general-turned-king in an RPG game. The brand vision and mission certainly are outdated. It takes away the individual's choice in today's job market in favour of fitting people into companies just for the sake of getting the economy to run like clockwork. Good luck, Joaquin. You're going to have a hard time getting clients to coach.

And here is another example of a poor personal brand persona. In fact, there is none to speak of. Julius thinks of himself as an employee first and foremost, and does not separate the private and the professional. He will not project a strong personal brand.

- Real name: Julius Doe
- Profession: Photographer
- Brand personality: Just being himself. There is no difference between the professional and the private.
- Brand name: Photographer
- Brand slogan: Strike a pose
- Brand voice: He always speaks naturally.

- Brand values: He follows his employer's values.
- Brand anti-values: He is not anti anything. He loves cameras, photographs and people.
- Brand visual identity: He dresses like everybody else.
- Brand vision: To be a good photographer.
- Brand mission: Executing tasks as instructed.

In this section, we have looked at the brand persona. We have seen how the principles of branding for companies can also be applied to personal branding. We have seen how personal brand persona building is predicated on the acceptance of us not seeing ourselves as employees of organisations only, but rather, as industry professionals. It is also predicated on us separating our private selves and our professional selves, and promoting our professional selves in our personal brand. We have used the "deeper reaper" method to depersonify ourselves in order to separate the private from the professional, and then to repersonify ourselves to begin building our personal brand. We have seen how our personal brand persona is at its root the amalgamation of archetypes. These archetypes will then be built up into a more comprehensive persona, including its brand name, slogan, personality, voice, values, anti-values, visual identity, vision and mission. In the next section, we will be taking a look at the next component of personal branding, namely competencies. Now that you know how to talk the talk, let's see how to walk the walk.

Competencies

A persona without accompanying competencies would defeat the purpose of personal branding. In fact, I would go so far as to say that it borders on fraud. In *Catch Me if You Can*, Leonardo DiCaprio plays the role of a con artist who creates multiple personas in order to scam others. The persona exists, but the requisite competencies are blatantly missing. He was just winging it, and letting the aura of the persona take him through all the characters he played. We, as professionals, cannot do that. Even if we were to be able to, it would not be sustainable. We need to build competencies up as much as we have built our personas up.

    Competency has three components, namely, knowledge, skills and attitude. This is the working definition of competency in instructional design. Knowledge is the information that we possess on a certain topic. We may know, for example, that project managers use a work breakdown structure to lay out the necessary tasks needed to meet project deliverables. We may know that project managers also use a Gantt chart to track timelines and milestone reporting. But are we able to create a work breakdown structure and a Gantt chart when we need to? That's where the skills come in. With skills, we should be able to create a suitable work breakdown structure and Gantt chart. With a deeper mastery of skills, we may even be able to merge these two together into one single project-monitoring document, and to customise it for the waterfall phases and the agile phases along our critical path. Attitudes are a more elusive concept. It refers to how we feel about the competency that we possess. Are we performing it mechanically step by step, or are we embodying it? Without a good attitude towards the area of competency, it would be very difficult to gain mastery. Imagine a digital marketer who knows how to navigate the Facebook ads manager. He knows how to get through each stop from setting the objectives to choosing the budget to choosing demographics. If he happens to think about digital marketing as a mere mechanical skill, he would only be able to execute as directed. He would not be able to make informed suggestions on the psychographics to be targeted. He would not be able to make informed suggestions on how to optimise the marketing expenditure so as to increase the click-through rate.

How do we develop competencies as a professional? Again, I'm going to be painting broad strokes here, with the step-by-step methods to be expounded in the later chapters. There are three parts to the development of competencies. The first is learning. Learning can be done in many ways. One could, for example, take a qualification in that particular skillset. One could also undergo apprenticeship, for skillsets that are more tactile in nature. Skills that require one to work with one's hands tend to be best learnt through apprenticeships. These include things such as shoemaking, car repair and carpentry. Aside from these more "traditional" routes of learning, there are also other means of learning that have surfaced since the 2000s. The first of these is learning through short courses. These short courses have become popular in many countries as a means of upskilling professionals and for professionals to switch careers into other industries. These do not require heavy investment in time and

The Conceptual Grounding of Personal Branding

money for the most part, and professionals are able to take on learning at a modular pace. One of the forerunners in this area is the Training and Education (TAE) Training Package endorsed by the Australian Industry and Skills Committee (AISC). There are also short courses offered through online learning platforms such as Udemy, Skillshare and Coursera, which can be undertaken by anyone, at any time, anywhere across the globe. These courses are offered by instructors from various countries, and are conducted through the method of "asynchronous e-learning" for the most part. Aside from that, practitioners in various industries have also created tons of video content on various topics – from music theory to Python coding – hosted on platforms such as YouTube, Nebula and Instagram Reels. For these creators, creating such content helps them in revenue generation through on-platform monetisation such as the YouTube Partner Program and direct monetisation methods such as "diamonds" on TikTok and KIK. Another reason they keep creating such content is for the purpose of search engine optimisation, especially if their videos are embedded via iframe onto the blog section of their own professional websites. For us, this content is especially useful for quick and cheap learning.

The second is practice. One needs to practise in copious amounts to develop one's competency. If one were to desire to become a university academic, one has to keep researching, writing and publishing as a form of practice, even as a graduate (or "postgraduate" if one were to be from the Commonwealth system) student. One cannot just write term papers and expect to become good at research and publication. An oft-cited statistic is that it takes 10,000 hours of practice to get good at a subject matter. We can't use that as a hard statistic, though, because it depends a lot on our pre-existing knowledge, transferable skills and personal abilities. If we were to have read up a fair bit about cinematography, we can expect to take a shorter time to get good in videography and video editing. If we were trained in Python, we can expect to take a shorter time to get good at JavaScript. Some of us are just naturally good with our hands, so any subject matter that involves tactile practice will not take very long for us to get good at.

The third is application. Application is key to developing competencies that allow a professional to practically apply these learnings to where they matter most, and to demonstrate their abilities in the area. More importantly, application allows the professional to build mastery over the subject matter, and to pick up tacit knowledge that he may not have been privy to. Learning and practice are formal knowledge. We pick up knowledge and practice skills from our learning takeaways. We build a certain level of command of the subject matter from knowledge and practice, but are far from being masters of that domain. Only with application can we truly approach mastery, because it puts us in real situations where that subject matter would be used. Only with application will we learn the things "on the ground", things that we could never have learnt in any classroom or online instructional materials. You see, tacit knowledge almost never makes it into any formal curriculum. It's hard to codify tacit knowledge and make it learnable. You just have to pick it up on the ground. A person could learn jazz theory from

The Conceptual Grounding of Personal Branding

YouTube videos, sure. He can get to know polyrhythms and polymeters very well, and learn how voice-leading works. But only with practice will he learn how to play polyrhythms and polymeters well without making them sound muddled. Only with practice will he learn how to choose chord voicings that use controlled dissonance effectively. But there's a limit to his competency. Unless he performs with other jazz musicians or in front of a live audience, he will never learn the tacit knowledge of the subject matter, such as the hand signs used to signal a key change, or how to read the audience's reaction to his rubato solo, or when to start and stop a "trading eights" section in an improv.

There are various levels of application, which provide different environmental conditions and stimulate different psychological states in professionals. The simplest level of application is the "safe environment". "Safe environment" applications are applications where there is little to no penalty for failure, and each failure is taken as a learning point. Such environments include classroom applications, simulations and guided applications. The professional is not under a whole lot of pressure, and consequently, the psychological state of the professional is less intense in such situations. The most intense and difficult level of application is immersive applications. This is when the professional is figuratively "thrown in the deep end" and has to not only apply the learning but also to learn from mistakes fast, and to make corrections on the fly where necessary. There are social and sometimes monetary penalties for failure in such environments. The professional is under a whole lot of pressure and the psychological state of the professional is highly under tension. Have you ever wondered why people can spend years learning a language through classroom means and only develop basic competency while another person can become much more proficient in that language in a short period of time if that person were to spend some time in the native country of that language? It is because in the classroom, the person can take failure for granted and not be pressured into performing optimally, while in that native country, the person is forced to learn quickly. To take their time in learning in the latter situation might lead to embarrassment, the inability to procure daily necessities or other penalties.

An example of how competencies are developed can be shown here. Joe is an accountant. He has grown rather tired of accountancy, and wishes to rebrand himself as a full stack web developer. He knows that these two subject matters are rather far apart, but he has been dabbling a little bit with web development since the early days of the internet. In developing competency, Joe has to bear in mind that he needs the knowledge. That is to say, he needs to know the languages that are needed to do front-end and back-end web development. Joe also needs the skills. He needs to know how to build a front-end (user side) website. He needs to know how to build a back-end on the server side. Together, this creates a dynamic website instead of a static one. He also needs to know how to build Application Program Interfaces (APIs) so that two unrelated front-ends can "speak to one another". Finally, Joe has to possess the right attitude. He cannot hope to undertake full stack web development using templates alone. He cannot have ambitions to simply build the same front-end and back-end every single time. He needs to cater each build to the needs of the product owner and the end user. Joe must internalise full stack web development to the extent that he is able to critically analyse the various nuances, problems and solutions that appear along the way.

Joe now has to develop his competencies. He decides to learn front-end languages first. He learns Hypertext Markup Language (HTML), Cascading Style Sheets (CSS) and JavaScript (JS) through YouTube. Plenty of tutorials there. He then decides to go onto Udemy to learn PHP and Python for the back-end, because the curriculum is more structured and thus has more learning efficiency. Joe is pretty confident about his learning. He thinks he knows enough to start practising. Joe practices by building a front-end and a back-end for himself first. The website is ugly and not quite user-friendly, but that's OK. Joe knows that he has no skills in UI/UX design anyway, so it is to be expected that his build is functional but not quite aesthetically pleasant. Most importantly, the website has a quick loading time, and is able to host all the necessary information he wants to be hosted. He tests it several times, and the back-end he built is able to support the front-end. Good job, Joe. Joe now has to start his application phase. This is the most daunting phase of all. He decides to start small. He asks a couple of his friends if he can build websites for them pro bono. Not all of his builds are successful. His friends give him feedback and he amends the front-ends and back-ends accordingly. Not too difficult. Joe now decides he should move out into a larger environment. He advertises his web development services on Fiverr, with a very low cost. A couple of people on a budget decide to engage his services. Now, "here comes the pain", as Al Pacino says in *Carlito's Way*. Should Joe be unable to deliver a front-end and back-end on time with the required quality, these new clients may make a claim to Fiverr for a refund. Worse, he might even get a bad review. And Joe knows how loud reviews can be these days. Reviews are the most informative way for future customers to size up the quality and trustworthiness of a service provider. Joe has stepped into the immersive zone. It's go time, and Joe floors the gas pedal.

The scenario above should serve as a template for us. Just as Joe did, we need to obtain the necessary knowledge and skills, coupled with the right attitude, if we are serious about obtaining competency in a certain subject area. To develop our competencies into something that the market will respect, as well as to support our personal brands, we need to learn, practise and apply. I cannot stress this enough. The more we apply what we have learnt and practised, the better we will get at the subject. We will develop mastery, as well as gain tacit knowledge. How did the professional poker player know when to call his opponent's bluff? How did the cop know that the suspect was lying? How did the designer know that two colour swatches would not match? Tacit knowledge. None of the above could ever be taught. You need to pick it up yourself through experience during application. In the next section, we will take a look at the final component of personal branding: storytelling.

Storytelling

Storytelling is traditionally not part of a company branding exercise. Brand stories aren't featured in a majority of brand books, but from time to time, we do get brands who create good backstories of their brand's founding, or how the founder's life experiences brought them to found that brand. Thus we have the example of Pampers, the brand of disposable diapers under Procter & Gamble's "house of brands". Pampers was invented by product researcher Victor Mills in 1956. He was none too happy about having to change his grandson's cloth diapers (which then had to be washed and dried) so he thought of a way to create disposable diapers.

However, I strongly advocate storytelling as a component in a personal branding exercise. No, storytelling is not about sitting around in a circle and reading a book to children. Storytelling is a methodology of presenting information so as to make it interesting, coherent and memorable. Think of it as the packaging for a product. Without the packaging, the product is just another product. The packaging is what brings out the brand and makes it attractive to customers. Don't underestimate the power of packaging design. Packaging design demonstrates the brand persona and product content (in your case, your competencies) very clearly. The audience is able to see what your personal brand and the product is clearly about, and can quickly decide on their own affinity with your brand. This is the reason why many countries have legislated plain packaging for cigarettes. Without branded packaging, new markets of potential smokers will not be attracted to try cigarettes based on the packaging design. Existing smokers will still stick to the brands they know but won't be tempted to try new ones.

We as humans find stories to be inherently interesting. Facts are just facts, but stories, that's a whole new level. But what is it about stories that attracts us? Well, stories are exciting. They are relatable. They are memorable. We were told stories as children and we've become accustomed to receiving information as stories. From the *Mahabharata* told in Indonesia and Indochina to Brer Rabbit told in America to the *Journey to the West* told in China and overseas Chinese diasporas to the Grimms' Fairy Tales told in Europe and much of the English-speaking world, we've grown to become very familiar with stories.

As we become adults, we continue to look for stories in everything we encounter in life. We love celebrity gossip because they're stories that we're interested in as adults. We look for the storyline in games like *The Witcher* and *The Last of Us*.

Imagine turning on Netflix and watching a movie that begins with a car chase. The car chase goes on and on through a tunnel with nothing else to see but the cars and the walls of the tunnel. This one continuous shot goes on for two straight hours. Would that be a movie we would want to watch? No. Why? Because there is no story there.

So, what is a story? A story is information packaged in a familiar plot structure and presented persuasively. Consider the following scenario. Jay went for a job interview. The interviewer asked him to say something about himself. And Jay goes:

"Hi, my name is Jay. I am a managerial accountant. I've been balancing balance sheets for many years. When I'm not balancing balance sheets, I like to go to the gym. I guess you could say I'm balancing work and life? That was just a little joke there. When I balance balance sheets, I make sure that the assets and liabilities are on par. Otherwise I might be held liable. That was another joke there. When I go to the gym I run on the treadmill. Although I balance the balance sheet, I'm not too fond of the balance beam in the gym. I don't know why. Maybe it's because I prefer to run. And I can't run on the balance beam. Well, I guess I can but it's too short to burn calories. And I might slip and hurt my ankle. Which reminds me, I'm flat-footed so I need high arch support in my shoes so that I don't hurt my ankle. Once I hurt my ankle so bad I couldn't run for a month. Anything else you'd like to know about me?"

Was that a story? Not really. It's just a mishmash of information presented randomly. It doesn't follow the methodology of storytelling that we have become accustomed to. In order for us to make use of storytelling effectively in our personal branding, we need to use the methods used by the stories that we have become familiar with since childhood. We need to organise the information about our brand according to familiar plot structures and present it persuasively. We will talk about this in turn.

The most basic plot structure is what is known as the "three-act structure". In every story, there must be a *setup*, a *conflict* and a *resolution*. The setup, as the name suggests, sets the audience up by painting a picture of the context of the story. In cinematography and filmmaking, the first shot that one sees of a scene is called the "establishing shot" for that very reason; it sets up the context for the scene. The story then proceeds towards more and more excitement, climaxing in the conflict. Now, there doesn't have to be a conflict in the sense of a fight or an argument. The conflict is just a term that we use to denote the point of highest tension or excitement in a story. And finally, that conflict must be resolved. Stories don't naturally stop at the point of the highest excitement. An exception to that is if the story is designed to end as a cliffhanger. For most of the time, the audience wants to see that the story ends nicely at a point of rest. We can see this plot movement in almost everything we read, hear or see. More elaborate stories would still use the three-act structure but might introduce multiple conflict points, false resolutions, or even leave space at the resolution for a continuation or sequel.

In novels and movies, we always encounter the context of the story first of all. Without the context, the audience may have trouble following the story. There will also be a point of highest tension or excitement. It might be where the protagonist and antagonist engage in battle. Or it might be where the hero tells the heroine he loves her. Whatever the genre of the novel or movie may be, we as the audience are always looking forward to this point of highest tension or excitement. But we don't want to be left there. As exciting as it may be, it is also uncomfortable for us. We want to be brought back to a point of rest, the resolution. That point of rest may be the protagonist emerging victorious, or the hero and heroine living happily ever after.

In music too, this three-act structure can be discerned. Harmonically, chord progressions typically move from the setup to the conflict to the resolution. In jazz, the most common chord progression, the II-V-I, follows this structure. The II chord serves as the setup, the V chord serves as the conflict and the I chord serves as the resolution. Of course, there can be many variations of this. Sometimes, the IV chord is substituted for the II chord (they're part of the same family). Sometimes the bII chord is substituted for the V chord (called the "tritone substitution"). But the main plot structure still remains. Similarly, the I-IV-I-V-IV-I structure in delta blues and the I-V-VI-IV chord progression in pop also feature the same structure. (Do note that I am following the standard of notation in jazz instead of the standard in classical music where minor chords are denoted with lowercase Roman numerals.)

This basic story plot can be further applied to and distilled into seven archetypal plots that surface again and again in all the stories we see, hear and read. These seven archetypal plots were discussed in great detail by Christopher Booker in his 2004 book, *The Seven Basic Plots: Why We Tell Stories*. His analysis was influenced greatly by Jung. In this book, I will refer to these "basic" plots as "archetypal plots" to give homage to Jung. Furthermore, the word "archetype" is a powerful term to analyse patterns of human behaviour for actionable insights. In fact, systems thinking also uses the word " archetypes", albeit in a different way. They use it to refer to the typical actions of humans in organisational settings, especially when there is a perceived benefit to oneself, or perceived competition.

These seven archetypal plots are:

1. Overcoming the Monster: This is where the protagonist is faced with a disruptive event or much stronger antagonist that disrupts his life. Initially uncertain of his fate, the protagonist decides to take the bull by its horns and comes out victorious.
2. Rebirth: This is where the protagonist encounters a sobering event, realises the error of his ways, and turns over a new leaf.
3. Quest: This is where the protagonist is sent on a critical mission, with dire consequences should he fail. The protagonist faces many challenges along the way, but returns with the prize.
4. Journey and Return: This is where the protagonist goes on a journey of discovery and returns much wiser than he was before.
5. Rags to Riches: This is where the protagonist starts off in a disadvantaged position, but unexpectedly gets a life-changing windfall.
6. Tragedy: This is where the protagonist experiences tragic event after tragic event in a downward spiral.
7. Comedy: This is where the protagonist goes through life always seeing the bright side and never aware of the ugliness that goes on around him. Even by the end of the story, he is still not aware of it.

In all the stories that we have encountered growing up, these archetypal plots have surfaced so many times that they have become deeply ingrained in us. We may not remember the

The Conceptual Grounding of Personal Branding

details of the stories which were presented in these plots but we sure are able to recognise the plot as soon as we see the story. Just look at the case of Jordan Belfort, the "Wolf of Wall Street" below. I am going to present publicly known facts about his life. Try to see if you can pick out the archetypal plots in his life story.

Jordan Belfort began his business career as a door-to-door meat and seafood salesman on Long Island, New York. His business didn't do too well, and he had to file for bankruptcy at the tender age of 25. Upon discovering that he could pump up cheap stocks and dump them when their stock prices rose, Belfort made tons of money trading these stocks. He became so rich that he could afford an extremely lavish lifestyle. Did you recognise the "rags to riches" plot in there? Easy peasy.

Belfort was subsequently indicted for securities fraud and money laundering in 1999. He served 22 months of a four-year sentence at the Taft Correctional Institution. While in prison, he met with comedian Tommy Chong, who encouraged him to become a motivational speaker. This encouragement was a huge inspiration to him. Belfort now travels around the world sharing his experiences and providing business analysis. Did you recognise the "rebirth" plot in there? Lemon squeezy.

Aside from the plot, every good story has to be narrated. The narration provides a means by which the audience not only recognises the plot, but is convinced of the information relayed in the story. But what goes into a good narration? Tone of voice? The words chosen? The grammar? The answer: all of the above.

All of the above can be summarised in the Greek modes of persuasion. Now, the Greek modes of persuasion are said to have come from the Ancient Greeks who would use these modes to convince others of their political philosophies. Today, they are used for a variety of purposes, from content writing to masterclasses, anywhere that good, strong persuasion is needed. There are five Greek modes of persuasion, each with its own virtues in adding persuasive value to the narrative.

1. Ethos: Persuasion built upon the credibility of the narrator. A narrator who has the expertise, authority and trustworthiness to narrate a story within his area of expertise will tend to be more persuasive than a narrator who doesn't. For example, a former convict who uses his experience to persuade others not to enter into a life of crime is using ethos as a mode of persuasion. Side note: Google's search engine algorithm acknowledges this. Google will not rank in its search engine any website that talks about any topic that it has neither expertise nor authority in, thereby affecting its trustworthiness.
2. Pathos: Persuasion built upon emotions through the use of imagery and words that are emotion-laden. For example, a donation drive for the poverty-stricken areas in Africa that makes use of images of ill and malnourished children is using pathos as a method of persuasion. Side note: Emotions are present in everything we do as humans. No matter how rational we want to be, we will always rely on our emotions to a certain degree. In marketing, for example, it is understood that people

will buy products emotionally but will try to justify it rationally.
3. Logos: Persuasion built upon logic. The narrative is strung together using logical reasoning. The most common logical formula used is the "if, then, else" formula. It states that if there is a certain condition or event that occurred, then it must hold a certain meaning or call for a certain action. Otherwise, it would mean something else, or require some other action. For example, "If my boss had told me earlier that the company was not doing well, then I would have agreed to take a paycut, otherwise, why would I?" Side note: Using logic doesn't always mean that the information is true. Logic only ties two pieces of information together with a causation relationship.
4. Kairos: Persuasion built upon the narrative's relationship to current conditions or trending topics. The narrative will thus be successful when delivered at the opportune moment. It would be at the "right place at the right time". For example, a narrative about the importance of flu vaccination delivered right after the annual flu season would be delivered at a very opportune moment. Side note: Using current conditions or trending topics is a very easy way to set up a "compare and contrast" scenario in the audience's mind.
5. Topos: Persuasion using an appropriate tone of voice that the audience would appreciate. For example, a narrative about mental health awareness delivered in an

empathetic tone would be using topos well. The same narrative told in a condescending tone of voice would not. Side note: The choice of an appropriate tone of voice is strongly influenced by cultural norms.

To sum up, the storytelling methodology can be used to deliver any information. By using storytelling, the information becomes more palatable and memorable. The storytelling methodology uses two main methods. First, a plot structure will be applied to the information to make it easier to consume. This is composed of the common three-act structure and an additional layer of the archetypal plots to direct the flow of the plot. Second, persuasive techniques will be applied to the information to make it more persuasive. Next, let's take a look at how we can tell our personal brands as stories using the storytelling methodology.

Storytelling for Personal Brands

The first thing that we have to understand is that storytelling is much more important to personal brands than it is to organisational brands. Why? Because when customers look at a company brand, they want to personify the brand "in the here and now". They only want to align with a brand whose image mirrors theirs at that moment in their lives. They will be quite happy to switch over to another brand should they feel that the earlier brand no longer mirrors their image. This is why we get ladies changing their preferences for clothing, hair and make-up brands as they move from their teenage years into adulthood and later years.

The Conceptual Grounding of Personal Branding

This is why we get people "growing out of" a certain fashion style, or a certain musical form.

This is also why we get people flocking to a brand that appeals to them without caring if that brand had a different target market in the past. Punks don't really care that Dr. Martens started off as a brand for old ladies with podiatric issues. They care that Dr. Martens carries an image now that suits theirs. Users of TikTok don't care that ByteDance, the company that created TikTok, used to create multiple lowbrow apps such as "Laugh So Much You'll Get Pregnant" and "Real Beauties: Everyday 100 Beautiful Girls". They only care that the ByteDance they know now has created TikTok with a brand persona that fits their personality.

In personal branding, on the other hand, the audience is never looking for the professional only as a "here and now". The affinity between the audience and the personal brand tends to be for a longer term than it is with a company brand. The audience wants to know what brought the professional to where he is. The experiences, motivations and learnings of the professional will all be taken into consideration in creating an affinity between the audience and the personal brand.

We thus need to develop a story for our personal brand, one that resonates well with our intended audience. Remember, our intended audience, in personal branding, are employers, clients and collaborators. If you are looking to appeal to people in the non-profit sector, your story has to appeal to the non-profit sector audience. If you are looking to appeal to the tech startup world, your story has to appeal to the tech startup audience. The audiences for these two purposes have different preferences for the stories they want to hear. The story is the packaging for the personal brand's persona and competencies. It envelopes, protects and presents the persona and competencies in a palatable, memorable and convincing manner.

Consider the following personal brand story by Jack. Jack writes: "Jack is known around the world as the best there is, the best there was and the best there ever will be. He is wise and experienced beyond his 25 years of age. He is a cybersecurity specialist, a part-time doctor and a lawyer to the celebrities in Hollywood. His skilled hands are able to perform the most intricate surgeries, his ears are tuned to perfect pitch and he has been known to make millions of dollars overnight on social media without making any effort or investing any capital at all. Jack is now looking for an internship opportunity at any firm."

Now, does that sound convincing to you? It sure doesn't! Why? Well, firstly, it is too fantastical. Jack is only 25 and is already the best around the world past, present and future? That does not make sense. Secondly, it is inconsistent. A cybersecurity specialist who is also a part-time doctor and a lawyer to the stars demonstrating his skill through perfect pitch and making money on social media? The performance does not fit the profile! Thirdly, it is questionable. A 25-year-old who claims to be a cybersecurity specialist, a part-time doctor and a lawyer surely must be too good to be true. They would have needed to undergo years of training for each skill that he claims to have. Would that have all fit within his tender 25 years of age? And making millions of dollars with no effort or money? Come on...

The Conceptual Grounding of Personal Branding

Consider this story next. Jen is 40 years old. She is an accountant. She did her Bachelor's degree in Accounting at McGill University. She has worked in several companies before. She is now looking for an accounting job.

Now, does that personal brand story sound convincing to you? Sure, it does. It seems highly possible. But would that convince you to trust in the brand image and the professional's competency? Absolutely not. The brand image is bland and looks like a cookie-cutter image. An accountant with an accounting degree looking for an accounting job. Dime a dozen. The competencies sound undeveloped and basic. A 40-year-old accountant with no major achievements looking for yet another accounting job? Did her skills remain the same as they were when she graduated? Has she not grown as a professional?

The intended target audience must be convinced of the story. In order to begin telling a convincing story, every personal brand has to first apply the three-act structure. Just as the three-act structure is ubiquitously seen, heard, read and watched in almost every movie, novel and piece of music we have encountered, the three-act structure should be used in every brand story. Setting your brand story up as a three-act structure helps both you and the audience. It helps you to set perimeters for your brand story such that you are conscious of the flow when you tell it. It helps the audience consume and remember the story because the three-act structure is just so familiar to the audience. It's like putting meat between two pieces of bread. Anywhere you go around the world, you know that it's a sandwich. This is how a personal brand story should be structured:

- Setup: How your personal brand began. For example, have you always been keen on your chosen profession even as a child? Or did your father play a major role in influencing you to take on this profession? Or did you fall in love with it after gaining some experience as an intern?
- Conflict: The key events that took place in the life of this brand. For example, what major clients have you worked with? What were your major achievements?
- Resolution: Where you are now, and what your plans are for the future. For example, what are you working on currently? What is your mission as a professional? What medium-term and long-term visions do you wish to achieve?

Consider this scenario, for example. John wanted to see how he could tell his personal brand story. He drafted out his three-act structure. This is how it read:

"John Doe began his career as a hotelier after a fateful visit to Ritz-Carlton. The professionalism, attention to detail and dedication to service caught his eye, and he knew he wanted to be a part of that. He pursued a diploma in hospitality management soon after and never looked back. As a hotelier, John has managed teams of over 100 service staff at one go. John was also a key player in setting up protocols for the teams under his management to follow. These protocols have saved the hotel almost $500,000 in shift overstaffing and waste perishables. John is planning to become a trainer for the butlering services. It is his

The Conceptual Grounding of Personal Branding

belief that in the hotel industry, there are no small roles, only small-hearted service persons."

As you can see, by applying the three-act structure, one's personal brand begins to take on a much more coherent form. This is because there is only so much that the intended target market can tell about a personal brand from its persona. They can tell whether the personal brand suits their own image, which then influences them to consider a certain affinity with the personal brand. They then would want to know what the professional holding that personal brand can do for them. This is where they would want to see the competencies that the professional holds. Should the professional possess the necessary competencies that fit their needs, they would find further affinity with the professional's personal brand. To cement this affinity, the brand story would need to be told. By packaging the persona and competencies in one convincing, palatable and memorable package, the professional convinces his audience that there is an affinity between themselves and his personal brand.

To develop the personal brand story further, the professional should then attempt to apply at least one of the archetypal plots. This adds so much more flavour to the three-act structure. The archetypal plots embed the three-act structure within it, and go further to direct the story flow as well as to add nuances to the three-act structure. The archetypal plot structure chosen will tell the personal brand story differently:

- Overcoming the Monster: As a professional, you faced a situation which could have potentially disrupted your professional life. But you took it head on, and emerged victorious.

- Rebirth: As a professional, you made some mistakes in the past. But you learnt from it and are now a completely new person.
- Quest: As a professional, your ambition and motivation drove you to search for skills or opportunities that most others would find elusive. You managed to find it, and now you wear it proudly as a badge of honour.
- Journey and Return: As a professional, you took some time for exploration and discovery. You learnt a lot during that time, and now you are equipped to share your experience with others.
- Rags to Riches: As a professional, you did not start off on the same level as others. But an opportunity came by and you seized the day. Now, you are in a better place than you were before.
- Tragedy: As a professional, you went on a downward spiral and you're now far worse than you were many years ago. Pro-tip: Don't use this archetypal plot unless you want to garner sympathy from your audience.
- Comedy: As a professional, nothing fazes you. You always and only see the bright side of life. You are positive beyond words, and take each day as it comes. Pro-tip: Don't use this archetypal plot unless you want to appeal to an audience that is only and exclusively interested in positive vibes (such as if you're applying to work with Ned Flanders from *The Simpsons*).

The Conceptual Grounding of Personal Branding

Remember John Doe from above? He wanted to add some pizzazz to his personal brand story. He rewrote his three-act structure in each of the archetypal plots to see which would be the most appropriate to use.

Overcoming the Monster: "John Doe began his career as a hotelier after a fateful visit to Ritz-Carlton. The professionalism, attention to detail and dedication to service caught his eye, and he knew he wanted to be a part of that. He pursued a diploma in hospitality management soon after and began work at Four Seasons. John rose through the ranks and was eventually given the task of managing teams of over 100 service staff at one go. On a fateful day on the way to work, John met with a terrible accident that left him unable to speak coherently. John persevered in his rehabilitation and recovered. His recovery brought him back stronger. During his downtime, John worked on setting up protocols to streamline business processes. These protocols saved the hotel almost $500,000 in shift overstaffing and wasted perishables. John now plans to become a trainer for the butlering services. It is his belief that in the hotel industry, without a challenge, there can be no success.

Rebirth: "John Doe began his career as a hotelier after a fateful visit to Ritz-Carlton. The professionalism, attention to detail and dedication to service caught his eye, and he knew he wanted to be a part of that. He pursued a diploma in hospitality management soon after and never looked back. Starting from the bottom, John rose up the ranks to manage teams of over 100 service staff at one go. John realised that good managers need to be trained and not just promoted into position after a mass walkout during one of his shifts. John decided to upskill and pick up agile management methods. He soon developed protocols for the teams under his management to follow. These protocols saved the hotel almost $500,000 in shift overstaffing and wasted perishables. John is planning to become a trainer for the butlering services. It is his belief that the best way to educate is by sharing his mistakes with others."

Quest: "John Doe began his career as a hotelier after a fateful visit to Ritz-Carlton. The professionalism, attention to detail and dedication to service caught his eye, and he knew he wanted to be a part of that. He pursued a diploma in hospitality management soon after and never looked back. John has managed teams of over 100 service staff at one go. John soon realised that he needed to skill himself up as a manager if he wanted to go far. He took a sabbatical and pursued a degree in hospitality management and human resource management. Upon returning to the hotel industry, John's key achievement was setting up protocols for the teams under his management to follow. These protocols saved the hotel almost $500,000 in shift overstaffing and waste perishables. John is planning to become a trainer for the butlering services. His personal motto is "Seek, and you shall find".

Journey and Return: "John Doe began his career as a hotelier after a fateful visit to Ritz-Carlton. The professionalism, attention to detail and dedication to service caught his eye, and he knew he wanted to be a part of that. He pursued a diploma in hospitality management soon after and began work at Four Seasons. His career growth was initially slow, and John left the industry to pursue a variety of other professions. John recently returned to the industry after amassing a multitude of management skills, especially people management. Equipped with these skills, John managed teams of over 100 service staff at one go and also set up protocols for the hotel. These protocols saved the hotel almost $500,000 in shift overstaffing and waste perishables. John is planning to become a trainer for the butlering services. It is his belief that absence makes the heart grow fonder.

Rags to Riches: "John Doe began his career as a hotelier after a fateful visit to Ritz-Carlton. The professionalism, attention to detail and dedication to service caught his eye, and he knew he wanted to be a part of that. He pursued a diploma in hospitality management soon after and began work at Four Seasons. John's career progression was initially slow, until he met a mentor who coached him on becoming a better hotelier. With that, John eventually managed teams of over 100 service staff at one go and set up protocols for the teams under his management to follow. These protocols saved the hotel almost $500,000 in shift overstaffing and waste perishables. John is planning to become a trainer for the butlering services. It is his belief that with the right coaching, anyone can become someone.

Tragedy: "John Doe began his career as a hotelier after a fateful visit to Ritz-Carlton. The professionalism, attention to detail and dedication to service caught his eye, and he knew he wanted to be a part of that. He pursued a diploma in hospitality management soon after and started work at Four Seasons. John's career progression was slow initially, and it was further hampered by an accident that left him unable to speak. John had to leave the hotel industry and eke out a living doing various odd jobs. John now hopes to become a trainer for the butlering services. It is his belief that one has to do what one has to do to survive.

Comedy: "John Doe began his career as a hotelier after a fateful visit to Ritz-Carlton. The professionalism, attention to detail and dedication to service caught his eye, and he knew he wanted to be a part of that. He pursued a diploma in hospitality management soon after and never looked back. John started from the bottom up and was happy to take his time learning as much as he could. He took everyday as it came, and even did an entire shift happily alone after his colleagues walked out on him. John was happy to help the hotel save some money with the simple systems he suggested. John is planning to become a trainer for the butlering services. It is his belief that one must always be happy in life and at work.

Which of these did you like best? Trick question. It's not up to you. It's up to John and what he wants to emphasise. John has to understand his potential employers and what story would resonate best with them. Now, all the information that John mentions in all those iterations of his brand story are true. None of them were fabricated. All he did was emphasise different events in the different archetypal plots.

After some reflection on the various hiring managers he has met over the years in the hotel industry, John evaluated all the archetypal plots that he wrote his brand story in. He decided to eliminate "comedy". "No self-respecting hospitality manager should be so happy-go-lucky," he thought to himself. "After all, hospitality is serious business." He decided to eliminate "tragedy" too. If there is one thing he knows about people, it is that people like to be negative, but they don't like to hear negativity from others. The tragedy plot was just too negative to be told. He wasn't sure that people would like to hear that kind of negativity.

He thought that "overcoming the monster", "rebirth", "quest", "journey and return", and "rags to riches" were all equally good. But he decided to go with "rags to riches" because he wanted to emphasise the mentorship he had as being a crucial component in his development as an industry professional. He also knew that people in the butlering services really hold mentors in high regard. "Maybe they're stuck on the idea of Alfred and Batman," he thought to himself, chuckling at his own wit.

John then decided to turn on the "Open to Work" badge on his LinkedIn and post the story on the "About" section of his profile. But since this story would be read by many potential employers, he would need to be more persuasive. John decided to apply the modes of persuasion to his story.

"John Doe began his career as a hotelier after a fateful visit to Ritz-Carlton. The professionalism, attention to detail and dedication to service caught his eye, and he knew he wanted to be a part of that. He pursued a diploma in hospitality management soon after and began work at Four Seasons. John's career progression was initially slow, until he met a mentor who selflessly coached him on becoming a better hotelier. Without his good mentorship, John could not have managed teams of over 100 service staff at one go and set up protocols for the teams under his

Rebrand Yourself, Retell Your Story

management to follow. These protocols saved the hotel almost $500,000 in shift overstaffing and waste perishables. John is now fully equipped to mentor others. He believes that there is no better place to mentor others than in the butlering services. In this era where people spend more time with their computers and devices than with others, the personal touch of the butler is desperately needed. It is his belief that with the right coaching, zeroes can become heroes."

Now, what did you think of that? Did you see how he reworded his brand story to apply ethos, pathos, logos, kairos and topos so that his story became more persuasive?

Ethos: "managed teams of over 100 service staff at one go and set up protocols for the teams under his management to follow. These protocols saved the hotel almost $500,000 in shift overstaffing and waste perishables"

Pathos: "mentor who selflessly coached him", "zeroes can become heroes"

Logos: "Without his good mentorship, John could not have managed teams"

Kairos: "In this era where people spend more time with their computers and devices than with others, the personal touch of the butler is desperately needed"

Topos: An authoritative yet empathetic tone of voice

Now, if you were a hiring manager in the butlering division of a major hotel, wouldn't you be convinced to hire John?

The Conceptual Grounding of Personal Branding

Taking stock

This chapter presented personal branding in a "whole-to-part" sequencing structure. The intention of this was to "front-load" the theoretical and conceptual grounding of personal branding before moving on to the subsequent chapters. By front-loading content, you, as the reader, will get a clear picture of the conceptual grounding of personal branding. You will be able to activate your mental curiosity to continually think about these concepts as we proceed to the other chapters.

The overall picture of personal branding was firstly presented. A definition of personal branding was given, and its relevance to the industry professional was clarified. The whole was then broken up into its parts for further conceptual explanation.

The first part of the whole that was explained was the concept of brand persona. I began by looking at brand archetypes, which would then be amalgamated into brand personalities. This personality would then be developed into a brand persona by way of the brand name, brand slogan, brand voice, brand values, brand anti-values, brand visual identity, brand vision and brand mission. The brand persona as a concept was first explained with reference to company branding, because that is how it is most predominantly used. This concept was then applied to personal branding. I showed how the concept of brand persona can just as easily be applied to personal branding as it is to company branding.

For personal branding, the prerequisite of creating a persona is to firstly agree to see oneself as an industry professional rather than just an employee of a company. Seeing oneself as an employee is disadvantageous because one tends to find too much comfort in the company rather than be aware of the developments in the larger market and industry. Finding comfort in the company, while in and of itself a good thing, may not motivate one to gain a competitive advantage against fellow professionals, stay relevant to the industry or maintain a mindset of resilience.

The second prerequisite is to agree that the professional and private sides of an individual should be separated, with the professional side being developed into the personal brand. In other words, the professional is not recommended to "be himself" as some management gurus might suggest. Being oneself is not healthy for the personal brand, because one's private side may not be taken well by the target market for one's professional side.

The professional who decides to engage in a personal branding exercise must then depersonify himself in order to clearly separate the private from the professional side. He then must repersonify himself by choosing one or more of the brand archetypes, just like how a company would if it were to undergo a branding exercise. The professional will then develop his personal brand persona by crafting and aligning all the components of his personal brand persona with the chosen archetype(s).

The second "part" of the personal branding "whole" is competencies. The components as well as the process of developing competency were established. Competency is made up of knowledge, skills and attitude. Only with these three present can one truly say that one is competent in a subject matter. One cannot

The Conceptual Grounding of Personal Branding

be competent with just knowledge alone. In the academic industry, such individuals are jokingly referred to as "armchair theorists". One cannot be competent with skills alone. One would not be able to utilise those skills creatively and cognitively with only skills. One cannot be competent with just a good attitude alone. One would not be able to stand up to any performance challenge. I then looked into how one can develop this competency. One has to learn, then practise, then apply. One can learn from a variety of sources, as long as those sources are teaching the correct information, and one can make sense of what is taught. One has to also practise copiously because it helps one retain the knowledge that one learnt. And one has to apply that practice into real-life situations. The closer to real life the application is, the better it would be for developing competency.

The third part of the whole is storytelling. While not being traditionally a component of company branding, storytelling is important in personal branding. Storytelling is the packaging for the persona and competencies. Telling the persona and competencies as a story makes it more palatable, convincing and memorable. In packaging the persona and competencies as a story, the professional should firstly set a structure for his personal brand persona and secondly, apply persuasive techniques. In terms of the structure, I have looked at the basic three-act structure, and expanded into the seven archetypal plots. I have explained how "Overcoming the Monster", "Rebirth", "Quest", "Journey and Return", "Rags to Riches", "Tragedy" and "Comedy" can be used to tell a personal brand story, to different effects. To make the personal brand story even more effective, the narrative should be delivered using the Greek modes of persuasion of ethos, pathos, logos, kairos and topos. These modes of persuasion can be employed independently of each other, but are most powerful when employed together.

Now that you know the conceptual framework for personal branding, we will continue on our "whole-to-part" journey. In the next chapter, I will explain the rationale behind personal branding. I will show how having a strong personal brand brings about several benefits, namely, allowing you to gain a competitive advantage, enabling you to stay relevant, helping you to mitigate the risks of "the many watching the many", building up your resilience in the event of any shocks to the industry and sending a clear signal to the industry amidst all the noise.

CHAPTER 3

The Benefits of Personal Branding

Personal branding is very important in today's business environment. In the days before the Industrial Revolution circa the 1760s, people thought of themselves as artisans and banded together in guilds. You can still see remnants of these guilds in certain locations such as Northamptonshire and Liverpool. When industrialisation became more entrenched around the 1840s, people started to see themselves as employees rather than artisans. Production-specific technical skills were most revered, as manufacturing and mining were the key drivers of the economy at that time. This change from a pre-industrial to an industrial economy led Karl Marx to study the effects of industrialisation and saw how people in industrialised economies became alienated from their product, the act of production, their species-being as humans and their colleagues. This was because under an industrialised economy, most people no longer owned the "means of production", unlike during the pre-industrial economy characterised by artisanship.

With the Second Industrial Revolution (also known as the Technical Revolution) from the late 19th century to the early 20th century, white-collar skills in management and service provision became revered. People began to think of themselves as PMEBs (professionals, managers, executives and businesspersons) or alternatively PMETs (professionals, managers, executives and technicians) but the emphasis on the organisation of employment was still important. Many people prided themselves on the offices they held in organisations, and loyalty to the organisation was held in high regard. In this era, people heralded the idea of staying in the same organisation for decades, with the hope of retiring comfortably with a pension.

The development of computing brought about the Third Industrial Revolution, sometimes referred to as the Digital Revolution, beginning in the late 20th century. The mentality of professionals shifted away from the organisation to their own individual ambitions. Professionals did not see the virtue of being employed for lengthy periods of time in organisations anymore. They would liberally leave organisations in favour of their professional ambitions, some taking to establishing new startups of their own, and others becoming project professionals in the gig economy, and yet others moving from organisation to organisation adding value with the skills they possess. Concurrently, the pension system was removed from many

The Benefits of Personal Branding

organisations. There was no longer a reason to stay for decades in the same organisation. Today, many (but not all) professionals think of themselves as "industry professionals" more than employees of an organisation. They are versatile, mobile and agile. And what enables them to be versatile, mobile and agile? Their personal brands.

A strong personal brand brings along with it many positive benefits. It also allows us, as industry professionals, to avoid some negative downsides in today's business world. No professional is an island. Professionals exist within an ecological environment. It is that environment that provides the necessary resources for that professional to survive. And if that environment changes, the professional too, must adapt to the changes. Living organisms adapt well to environmental changes. Cats and pigs quite easily adapt to domesticated and wild environments. In a wild environment, their bodies and minds change to adapt to it. In a domestic environment, they will adapt physically and mentally too. The advantages listed for having a personal brand in this chapter relate the industry professional closely to his environment. Having a personal brand enables the industry professional to not only survive in, but to furthermore thrive in the industry and market.

Now, the advantages I identify here are neither exhaustive nor mutually exclusive. When you create and maintain your own personal brand, you might find that there are more benefits to be had. Also, the benefits discussed below do have overlaps with each other.

Gaining a competitive advantage

Firstly, personal branding helps us get a competitive advantage vis-a-vis other professionals. Just as it is with companies, in the world of business, other similar professionals could be competitors or collaborators. They could even be our clients, if we're selling a B2B model, or if we're in a subcontracting relationship with them. As an organism, we're always competing for resources with others of the same species. When the environment is full of resources, such as in a "blue ocean", we all have enough space between ourselves to live comfortably. When the environment has too few resources, we would have to compete for these resources. It might end up as a "red ocean", where we're all driven to become ruthless just to get available resources. Or we might end up collaborating with each other for collective benefit, capitalising on each other's strengths.

To be honest, the "red ocean", "blue ocean" scenario applies most directly to companies which are in perfect competition with each other. When companies are in perfect competition, they compete based on price, quantity and quality. The customer will look out for the company that has the cheapest price with the largest quantity and the best quality. Price is always the compounding factor here. Customers will always reduce the quantity and quality to a price quotient. Imagine this familiar scenario: Two ice-cream sellers along the beach within sight of all the customers. Both of them must price their ice-creams at the same price. Should one drop the price of his, the other one has to either drop his price too, or serve larger scoops, or offer a more premium flavour of ice-cream. The same thing applies

The Benefits of Personal Branding

to professionals. Professionals who merely market their skills and experience with no personal brand are all engaging in perfect competition with each other. Imagine this scenario. Two professionals with the same skills and experience go to a job interview for the same position. Who would get employed? Why, the one with the lower expected salary, of course. Two professionals with the same skills and experience bid for a project. Who would win the bid? The one with the lower price quote, of course.

The primary virtue of personal branding is that it takes us out of the price war. Those who primarily consider themselves only as employees can jolly well continue to fight the price war. Whenever they switch jobs, they will carry along their last drawn salary, their qualifications and their experience. The hiring companies will choose the potential employee with the lower last drawn salary, most appropriate qualifications and most relevant experience.

With a personal brand, we are instead carving niches for ourselves that are price-inelastic. That is to say, with a personal brand, whatever price we are asking for does not matter. Potential employers, clients and collaborators will choose to work with us based on how close our persona is to their own personalities (be it their own individual personality or their company's brand personality), how useful our competencies are and how our story speaks to them.

Consider this scenario: Jacob put up a job ad. He's looking for someone to join him as a digital marketing manager. Three people respond to the job ad.

Rebrand Yourself, Retell Your Story

The first candidate sends in his resume. Resume looks good. No section on career highlights, but at least he listed his qualifications and experience clearly. Jacob invites this person for an interview. They meet. The candidate says "I am trained in digital marketing. I have five years of experience. My last drawn pay was $4,500. I'm asking for $5,000 remuneration now. I will work as hard for you as I did for my current and previous employers." Jacob keeps this in mind.

The second candidate sends in his resume. Resume looks good. No section on career highlights, but at least he listed his qualifications and experience clearly. Jacob invites this person for an interview. They meet. The candidate says "I am trained in digital marketing. I have five years of experience. My last drawn pay was $4,000. I'm asking for $4,500 remuneration now. I will work as hard for you as I did for my current and previous employers." Jacob keeps this in mind. The second candidate seems a better choice than the first. He's asking for less with the same qualifications and experience.

The third candidate sends in his resume. Resume looks good. Career highlights are impressive. He has had some struggles in the past but managed to overcome them. Sounds like a fighter. The company has had some trouble with going to market as of late. Jacob needs someone who can fight tooth and nail to bring the product to market, build brand awareness and drive digital sales conversions. This candidate skilled himself up proactively and served some pretty big names too. Impressive. The company needs someone proactive. The company cannot do with just someone who executes pay-per-click marketing without being proactive with the marketing optimisation. Jacob invites this person for an interview. They meet. The candidate has this air about him. Not a bad air. Just different. He dresses and speaks well, but there are tiny nuances about him that suggest he's a little bit caustic. The candidate says, "I am trained in digital marketing and I have five years of experience. But that's not what you should know about me. I experiment with new methods of digital marketing. I don't take the beaten path. I can be quite ruthless when it comes to keyword bidding. I'm not completely fond of automated marketing because I don't have complete control over the process. I'm always on the lookout for influencers who I can use for influencer marketing. And I'm not averse to guerrilla marketing tactics, even if it sits in the grey area of legality and ethics. I'm asking for $5,500." Jacob is sold. He doesn't need a digital marketer who plays by the rules all the time. Some companies might. Not Jacob's company. They need someone bold, daring and brave to take command of the marketing strategy. Jacob decides to make an offer to the third candidate.

The VRIO framework used in business modelling clarifies this idea of competitive advantage, which we can adapt and apply to personal branding. It defines four components of competitive advantage, and only with all four components met can an organisation or professional obtain competitive advantage. The four components are:

- Value: Is the professional able to carve out a niche for himself such that he has control of that space without much interference from other competitors?

- Rarity: Is the professional able to establish a sense of uniqueness about himself via his persona, competencies and story?
- Imitability: Would it be easy to imitate the professional's personal brand?
- Organisation: Is the professional able to organise himself such that he can live up to his brand? This means that his competencies (knowledge, skills and attitude) must be able to live up to the persona, and that the story he builds from the present to the future is a sequel to the story that he told of his past to his present.

The third candidate in the scenario above meets all the components of VRIO.

- Value: The third candidate is able to carve out a niche for himself. He doesn't take the beaten path in digital marketing. He is always on the lookout for suitable influencers. He is not averse to guerrilla tactics.
- Rarity: The third candidate is able to establish a sense of uniqueness about himself. It's not often that one meets a digital marketer who is experimental in marketing.
- Imitability: It would not be easy to imitate the professional's personal brand. The persona, combined with the tacit knowledge and attitude that he has (as part of his competency in digital marketing) as well as his brand story is not something that someone can make up in a short period of time

- Organisation: The third candidate is able to organise himself to execute his persona, competencies and story in synthesis with each other. He found for himself an organisation that has affinity with his personal brand. This organisation will be the one providing him with the resources he needs to thrive as an industry professional.

Staying relevant

The second advantage of personal branding is that it helps us stay relevant in the business environment. If we were to think of ourselves only as employees, we might be lulled by the comforts that our company of employment provides us. We might make it a priority to keep our bosses happy only, because making our bosses happy guarantees us continued employment. We won't see the need to look outside our companies of employment. Our companies shelter us from the rain and effectively become the hands that feed. But what happens when that shelter is shaken and the hand that feeds cannot feed anymore? Our professional worth might go down with it. We might have become too rooted in and attached to the company to see that there is a greater environment outside the company. In ecological terms, the company has become the host, and we have become the parasite. (I know the word "parasite" is not a nice word to use in regular parlance, but trust me, it doesn't have the same connotations in the discipline of ecology.)

By constantly keeping our personal brand in mind, we are always looking at the wider industry, instead of simply inward to our companies of employment. The wider industry is the one providing us with resources, and when it changes, we will be aware that we need to accordingly change as well. The business environment of today has changed so much from the past. Furthermore, the pace of change today is so much more rapid than it was previously. In the (relatively) distant past, managers need not bother with computer work. They could get their staff to perform spreadsheet tasks, type out reports and create presentations. We still do see a small number of older C-suite executives who still need a personal assistant and still dictate their letters to a secretary who types it out for them.

But these practices are few and far between these days. With the development of business technologies, managers now can and must schedule their own appointments in shared calendars. Managers now must work with software to vet and review their staff's work. They need to update staff movement platforms and project management platforms. Business technologies are developing at a much more rapid pace than in the past. And I'm not just talking about the changes between the Technological Revolution and the Digital Revolution. Even within the digital era itself, the changes in the years since the Digital Revolution have themselves been rapid. Years ago, there was only MySpace, Friendster and the lesser known Multiply as the predominant social media platforms for users to share their content with the world. Today, social media platforms compete to outdo each other on a daily basis; not just for users but for marketing purposes as well. They change their promotion and recommendation algorithms constantly and come up with new products and

The Benefits of Personal Branding

features so that their platforms remain relevant to users. When their platforms remain relevant, advertisers will continue to use their platforms for marketing.

Consider the following scenarios:

James has a good job. He's been with the company for fifteen years. Everyday, James goes to work and does his job like a good employee. He keeps his head down, and does not want to offend the bosses. After all, his livelihood depends on his continued employment. James executes his duties dutifully. Whatever is important to his bosses, James prioritises. Whatever isn't, James doesn't quite bother with. James likes his colleagues, but does not want to get involved in office politics. One day, James' bosses break some terrible news to the employees. The company has to shut its doors. Business has not been great. James is sad to go, but what other choice does he have? He goes onto job portals and is shocked to find that employers are now looking for applicants with a lot more skills than he has. He was caught unawares.

Jordan has a good job. He's been with the company for 15 years. Every day, Jordan goes to work and does his job. He is proactive in making suggestions for business improvement, and at times he has clashed with his bosses on the direction of the company. He feels that it is his duty as an industry professional to make informed suggestions whether his bosses like it or not. James executes his duties diligently. Whatever is important to his bosses, James prioritises. Whatever isn't, James keeps his eye on. "What is not important today may be important tomorrow", James rationalises. He keeps abreast of what is important in other companies by talking to his friends and following up on trends in the industry. James notices that there are new business softwares being continually released, which are much more powerful than the ones he has been using. James acknowledges that with the development of technology, some business technologies may be retired and replaced by new ones. James tries to pick up these new software skills through watching YouTube videos and practising on his own through the trial versions. James does not want to get involved in office politics but keeps his ears open. The grapevine may have lots of noise, but one can discern signals from there too. One day, Jordan's bosses break some terrible news to the employees. The company has to shut its doors. Business has not been great. Jordan is sad to go, but what other choice does he have? He views job portals and finds that employers are now looking for applicants with different skillsets than what he started off with. He is not all that surprised. He has had whiffs of that scent from keeping in touch with industry developments.

James and Jordan are extreme examples of those who consider themselves as "employees" and as "industry professionals" respectively. James was caught unawares, while Jordan saw it coming. You see, in risk management, there is something called "conditional risks". These are technically called "aleatoric risks" and "epistemic risks" (there's a slight technical difference between the two), and we can be put at risk by conditions that develop that we are unaware of. We become unsure how affected we will be by these conditional developments, and we also are not sure how to react to these developments. James was at risk, and now his risk has become a real issue that he has to handle. Jordan was not at risk, because he kept abreast of industry developments. Now that he has to look for a new job, he is prepared. He knows that he will be affected by the conditions that developed over time, and he knows how he should react to them. He prepared himself by not just keeping abreast of industry news, but also by developing new skills along the way.

Mitigating the risks of "the many watching the many"

I really would like to teach the world to sing in perfect harmony, as the old Coca-Cola campaign from the 1980s says. Positivity is a good thing to believe in. But as any experienced project manager will tell you, there is positivity, and then there is the cold hard truth. There are negativities in this world that we must contend with as much as we want to believe in positivity. To not acknowledge these negativities will put us at risk. A strong personal brand helps us identify, assess and respond to these negativities.

A strong personal brand helps us mitigate the risks associated with "the many watching the many". Today's world of social media exposes us all to being under the watchful eyes of others. We are all watching each other. Thus, the many watching the many. This is going to continue well into the future, with blockchain technologies allowing us to see each other's digital wallets (such as MetaMask, Phantom and the like) and transactions. Once we set up a digital wallet and make purchases or sell items, everyone can see our wallet number and the transactions associated with this wallet. This situation of "the many watching the many" developed with the advent of Web 2.0, where internet participation became defined by user contributions and real-time interaction among users. There is a blurring of lines between internet users and content creators, with users being able to create content easily and cheaply, and content creators themselves playing the role of users. This departs significantly from yesteryear. In 1975, sociologist Michel Foucault noted that the modern age was characterised by "the few watching the many" while the pre-industrial age was characterised by "the many watching the few" (in his book *Discipline and Punish: The Birth of the Prison*). What he meant was that in the past, before industrialisation, any major crimes would subject the perpetrator to public shaming and public punishment. He might be paraded across the town tarred and feathered, or he might be drawn and quartered in the public square. The crucifixion of Jesus is a prime example of this. Jesus was publicly made to carry the cross he was to be hung upon while wearing a crown of thorns while everyone watched, jeered and hurled curses and projectiles. The public ("the many") would watch the few, who were found guilty of crimes, receive their (seemingly) just deserts. Enter the modern age. The age where cameras served as the eyes and ears of the few in power. Cameras allow the few to watch the many, giving rise to the phrase "big brother is watching". Today, with social media, everyone is watching everyone else. Any cultural transgressions, whether intentional or otherwise, can have severe repercussions. These cultural transgressions include any textual, graphic, videographic or sonic evidence of a person acting untowardly towards religious groups, women, ethnic groups, people of other sexualities and the like. Intentional or otherwise, the repercussions are a real threat. Professionals have lost their jobs, reputations, livelihoods and even lives as a result of these repercussions. And it is this threat that we want to mitigate.

This situation is exacerbated by the mindset of blame that has pervaded the "cancel culture" of today. This is, unfortunately, an unintended consequence of the progress of equality in the digital age. Back in the days when equality was but a mirage, there was a prevalence of "blaming the victim". In those days, a woman who was raped, for example, was barraged with a whole host of blame for being a victim. "She should not have dressed that way," some might say. "She should not have been out late at night without a chaperone," others might say. These statements are all unfair to the victim, because they all suggest that the victim was "asking for it". Similarly, a minority who was lynched was barraged with statements such as "He should not have been in that area" or "He should not have triggered them". These are similarly unfair because they place the blame on the victim.

Now, in the drive towards equality, society and social media should have stopped at exactly that. Equality. Everyone gets treated equally. Couple that with "equity" where everyone is treated fairly and we have a winner winner chicken dinner. But no, society and social media had to move to the opposite end. Instead of "blaming the victim", society and social media now is "blaming the offender". Whenever a woman is offended by a man's words (no matter how mild or extreme) on social media, these days no one asks the intention of the man. They immediately say, "He shouldn't have said that." Or, "He should not have said it that way." Or, "He should not have used that tone of voice." Anything to justify why the offended is correct in feeling offended. Whenever a minority is offended by a majority's actions, these days no one bothers to ask what the context was for the action to happen. They immediately say, "He shouldn't have done that." Or, "That is uncalled for." Or, "That is wrong, period." Anything to justify why the offended is correct in feeling offended. Oh, sure, the offender should not have said this or done that *after the fact*. But what if the other party was not offended, eh? Should the offender still not have said this or done that? Or would the actions and words not matter in that case? Somehow, though, the ones who are blaming the offender are pretty certain that they won't offend others, because they're so, you know, "woke". But the truth is, in this mindset of "blaming the offender", all of us have an equal chance of being an "offender" and being blamed. And, I repeat, this is what we want to avoid because this "blaming the offender" mentality can really hurt our professional reputation greatly.

So how does having a personal brand mitigate the risks of "the many watching the many"? Having a personal brand requires us to develop a persona around our professional selves. We are constantly reminded to maintain that persona so as not to "break kayfabe", as they say in professional wrestling. Of special importance are our brand values and brand anti-values. The brand values that we maintain keep us within the limits of our brand, while the brand anti-values remind us where we should not tread. Whatever activities we do in our professional capacities should maintain our brand values and brand anti-values. Whatever we do in private should be assessed in relation to our personal brand values so that it doesn't step into anti-values territory and consequently go off-brand.

Consider the following scenarios:

Jonah is a professor at a local college. He teaches engineering. His students expect him to be knowledgeable, wise and empathetic towards their learning. Jonah is also a jovial character and comes across as approachable. We could say that in the eyes of the public, Jonah is a Sage and a Caregiver. Now, Jonah is happy with how the public views his personal brand. He promotes the values of co-creation of knowledge, empathetic learning and personal mentoring. On the flip side, his anti-values are didactic learning, abuse of authority and academic elitism.

Now, unbeknownst to those who face his personal brand, Jonah is not a professor at home. He doesn't live that brand 24/7. When Jonah is with his friends, he becomes a frat boy. He curses like a sailor, he chugs beer right out of the keg and of course, he goes to parties. Jonah knows that whatever he does in private may very well be at odds with his professional persona. His actions may be misconstrued as being off-brand. He knows that in the age of the many watching the many, judgement lies in the court of public opinion. He does not wish to have to justify his private life in relation to his professional life. So what does Jonah do? Jonah makes sure that he only partakes in private affairs with friends who understand the importance of keeping the private away from the professional. Friends who won't take photos of him in a drunken stupor or shoot a video of him berating a friend jokingly (which is not uncommon, really). Friends who won't tag him in social media or let the world know of his private life.

There have been many instances where the court of public opinion has looked unfavourably upon a person's professionalism simply based upon that person's private life. We all know that what we do in private should have no bearing upon what we do professionally. Yet, the court of public opinion does not seem to think so. Why is that? Because they develop an image of us as professionals and come to expect certain ways of thinking, attitudes and actions from that very image. In other words, the public imposes a persona on us even if we don't have a persona that we present to them. And whenever any aspect of our private life becomes publicly known, the court of public opinion will judge that aspect. If it fits into their expectations of our persona, Saul Goodman ("it's all good, man"). If it goes against their expectations, it won't bode well for our professional selves. The public will feel a sense of cognitive dissonance whereby what they expected from us has been overturned. Cognitive dissonance is an unpleasant feeling to most people and they will react strongly against it. To put it very bluntly, when it comes to the private-professional divide, "the only crime is getting judged".

Joseph is a teacher at a public high school. He likes his job, but does find the students trying sometimes. He can deal with those who are less bright but display a desire to learn, but he is not too fond of those who have no desire to learn and

The Benefits of Personal Branding

clown around in class. Joseph is not aware of personal branding, so anytime anyone asks him what he does for a living, he says that he is a teacher at a public high school. Joseph performs his duties diligently, day in and day out. The teaching, the administration, the parent-teacher meetings all are performed to the best of his ability. Joseph presents himself like any other teacher. He uses the same language and tone of voice as they do. He wears the same clothes as they do. One day, a particularly mischievous student did something that really rubbed Joseph the wrong way. Joseph stormed out of class, dragged one of his colleagues out into the hallway and ranted. He was so mad that he didn't know how loud he was. His face turned red as he was describing the mischief that the student was up to, and expletives poured liberally out. Unbeknownst to him, another student around the corner was passing by. This student whipped out her mobile phone and recorded the entire episode. That video clip did not show the circumstances in the lead-up to this rant. It just showed the rant. This student cheekily uploaded this clip onto her TikTok with the title "Teacher loses his mind". It went viral. It was shared across TikTok. It was sent across WhatsApp. It even made its way onto Instagram Reels. Parents across the city saw it, and wrote in complaints to the school. They felt that Joseph's use of expletives was unbecoming of a teacher. They felt that Joseph was going to be a bad example to their children. The school fired Joseph. Joseph's professional worth vanished along with the firing. He was no longer a teacher at a public high school. He became just another person with a teaching diploma looking for a new job.

Aside from Jonah and Joseph's case, can any of us effectively merge our private and professional lives in our personal brand? The answer is: only if our private lives do not encroach onto our personal brand anti-values. There are situations where this can happen. If we are known in our professional brand to possess the archetypal qualities of the Ruler, such as if we were to be an extremely strict officer in the military who does not take ill discipline lightly, and we are also similarly strict in private, expecting our families and friends to be disciplined in their daily affairs, then we can merge our private and professional selves together. If we are a flamboyant fashionista who possesses the archetypal qualities of the Lover, and we similarly exude that same flamboyance at home and with friends, then we can merge our private and professional selves together. But that is not always the case. The industries and professionals we are in do not always support the same archetypes that our private selves are characterised by. For example, a flamboyant, rule-bending teacher like Great Teacher Onizuka is not always accepted in real life because the private side of Great Teacher Onizuka violates what the audience expects from teachers. In the anime, he is often seen prioritising his students' learning in and out of the classroom, even if it means flouting school rules and societal norms.

Building resilience

There is an adage in the business world that "change is the only thing that is constant". The truth of this statement cannot be overstated. The business world has changed greatly since the advent of the Digital Revolution. The business world today continues to change rapidly. New job roles are created to replace older job roles. New business softwares are being released constantly. Softwares are constantly being updated with new features so as to remain competitive and relevant in the industry. New skills are required, and old skills are retired. In risk management terms, we can thus say that the "conditions" for each industry and profession are developing so rapidly that if we do not keep abreast of the changes, we might be caught in a situation in the future where we're so far away from what the industry has become that we don't know our position, and we don't know how to navigate around the industry anymore. Having a personal brand helps remind us that we need to stay in touch, and this was covered above under staying relevant.

Now, what if something worse happens? In risk management, aside from "conditional risks", there are also "event risks". Event risks do not develop over time. They just happen. Some event risks we can foresee. For example, while we are executing the deliverables of a certain project, the client might ask for a revision. That is to be expected because it happens more often than not. Almost no client accepts our final submissions flat out. We can expect to see it coming within two weeks of the final submission of deliverables. Some event risks we cannot foresee. And these are the ones that can really throw a spanner in the works. Risk managers term those that are completely unexpected as "black swans". They're so unexpected, the probability of them occurring and the impact they might have on us are so completely alien to us. More often than not, however, we will encounter "dragon kings", events that are unexpected but we have a clue what they are. Covid-19 is one example of a dragon king. We know that there have been flu pandemics before, with the Spanish Flu (1918–1920), SARS (2002–2004) and the like. Of course we can expect there to be another flu pandemic. We just didn't know when it would hit, and the impact it would have on us. Covid-19 had a huge impact on economies around the world. The tourist economy was halted, and along with it, the airline and hotel industries. The F&B and retail industries lost a lot of business from the lockdowns, social distancing and other measures imposed to curb the spread of the disease. Some businesses closed down. Others had to pivot to other product offerings. Yet others were forced to change their business model by going digital, changing from B2C to B2B, and such. Employees in these industries were put on long leave, or were converted from a "contract of service" to a "contract for service", or simply lost their jobs.

Now, Covid-19 is not the only dragon king we face. There are a multitude of other event risks that could happen in our industries that force us out of our comfort zones. Industries outsourcing production to countries with cheaper labour and cheaper rent is another familiar dragon king. Dr. Martens famously partnered with NPS Shoes from 1959 to the mid-1990s when the former decided to outsource its production to countries in Asia where labour and land was cheaper. NPS Shoes was then forced to create its own brand, Solovair, in order to continue its business. So did many electronics manufacturers. So did many silicon chip manufacturers. So did many clothing manufacturers.

The Benefits of Personal Branding

Consider the following scenarios:

Jonathan was a regional sales director for a multi-national corporation. He worked hard to get to where he was. He made sure his sales team brought in revenues that exceeded the expectations of senior management year after year. He was excellent in reviewing sales canvases, and honing customer personas to target quality leads. He was great in mentoring his sales team in their pitching, and tightening areas of their sales scripts where objections were responded to. He sent his team on professional development courses to learn about cross-cultural selling and post-sales follow-ups. He was a skilled salesman, and an even more skilled sales manager. Unfortunately for him though, the company he worked for was looking to outsource production to countries where labour and rent were cheaper. They were looking to consolidate production, warehousing and sales to these countries. And they were not alone. Many of their competitors were looking to do so as well. That would mean that the company would downsize. Jonathan was retrenched. His services were no longer needed by the company. One would imagine that Jonathan could easily find another job as a sales director in any other company, right? Unfortunately not. Jonathan had spent way too many years in that one industry, and as a result, his sales skills were limited to the products of that industry only. Did he have any product knowledge about other industries? No. Were his sales skills transferable to other industries? Only in limited amounts. Jonathan had trouble looking for another job as a sales director with the same last-drawn salary. He was offered sales jobs, no doubt, but because of his lack of experience, he was not offered a salary that was matched to his last drawn. Jonathan was in a conundrum. He could accept those jobs, with a lower pay, but his mind kept thinking about his value and that he should be paid more than what they were offering him. He could hold out until a more suitable job with a more commensurate salary came along, but for how long? The lifestyle that he used to be able to afford with his salary (including commission) was not sustainable anymore. He had to live within lesser means now, and tighten the proverbial belt. Jonathan decided to take on a sales manager job in a different industry but didn't last long. They were selling products he was unfamiliar with, and he could not make the sales target that was given to his team. Further, the pay was nowhere near what he used to have. He had to drag himself into the office day after day. His mood became foul. He felt caged and helpless. Of course, he didn't last long. Eventually, Jonathan decided that he would just drive a private hire car to make ends meet, while waiting for an opportunity to assume a more suitable sales director position. It wasn't much, but he was assuaged by the thought that private car hire was a transient phase.

Jeff used to manage a plastics manufacturing firm. He rose up the ranks, starting off as a manufacturing assistant and eventually becoming General Manager. He made sure that all safety procedures were adhered to. He made sure that shifts were scheduled fairly and realistically. He made sure that inventories were kept in order. At a certain point in time, Jeff was retrenched. Plastics manufacturing was just getting too expensive in his city. It was just simply too expensive for plastics firms to afford the rent and the labour costs. The standard of living in his city was rising, you see. It made more sense for plastics manufacturers to relocate to areas where land and labour were both cheaper. It made more sense from a cost perspective. Jeff was out once again in the job market. He knew all there was to know about plastics manufacturing. He knew all there was to know about managing a plastics manufacturing firm. At one glance, he could see how schedules, inventories, warehousing and distribution fit into each other. He saw things from a process point of view. He could tell you which part of the process was kinked and needed to be straightened out. Yet, plastics manufacturing was on its way out. In fact, manufacturing was on its way out. Warehouses were shutting down. Factories were relocating. Factory workers were out of jobs and had to take on other below-professional jobs such as mall security and janitorial roles. Jeff had the skills but there was no market for his skills anymore.

What could Jonathan and Jeff have done in the situations they were in? An industry professional with a strong personal brand would resiliently rebrand if he were to be in that situation. He would be constantly reminded that he needs to be aware of the market demand and changes in the market and industry. He would refresh his brand constantly by adding on software skills, management skills or other technical skills to his set of competencies to meet minor changes in the industry. He would continually refresh his story to keep the market interested. For major changes in the industry, such as where dragon kings occur, he would rebrand.

Rebrand Yourself, Retell Your Story

The process of rebranding requires the professional to begin the branding process all over again. It requires him to relook his brand persona, competencies and storytelling. Moreover, it requires him to reassess the relevance of his former brand in relation to the new brand. He might choose to retire the former brand completely. He might choose to incorporate the former brand into the new brand. Or he might decide to put the former brand into hibernation, to be woken up at a later date when it once again becomes useful.

Take a look at the following scenario. Julian had been working in clothing manufacturing for 15 years. He was trained in business, and had worked in several clothing manufacturing factories in the areas of quality control, quality assurance and product development. Clothing manufacturing as an industry was facing issues. Consumer tastes had shifted towards fast fashion, and consumers had become less keen on quality clothing, in favour of cheaper clothing made with cheaper materials that would allow them to purchase and discard clothing in quick response to changing fashion trends. Julian knew that one day, something big might happen, but was not sure what or when. Eventually, the clothing manufacturers in his town decided to shift their business elsewhere. They looked for cheaper labour and cheaper rent overseas in response to the increasing demand for fast fashion. With almost all the factories in the town shutting down and shifting operations overseas, Julian knew he had to rebrand. He thought to himself, "What can I rebrand myself as? My professional status as a clothing executive is no longer relevant." Julian decided to do something different but related.

The Benefits of Personal Branding

He looked up his options and found something that he wanted to attempt. He was going to open an online clothing store. But there were already some competitors in that space. How was he going to differentiate himself from these competitors? Should he offer the same clothes at a lower price to gain an edge? No, he thought. That would be too risky. What if the competitors found an even cheaper supplier some time in the future? He would have to again reduce his prices. It was a rabbit hole he didn't want to go down. He decided to carve a niche for his brand. He first decided on his target market and their tastes. He could go for the goth kids, that would be fine. There was a significant number of goth kids in his town and the neighbouring towns, always moping around, wearing black and listening to depressing songs. He could go for the cute aesthetic too. Lots of kids in this town getting increasingly influenced by the cutesy scenes in Japan and Korea. He decided to go for the cutesy aesthetic. He looked up how the cutesy scenes displayed their graphics, illustration and photographs. He looked up the tone of voice and words they use. He felt confident at being able to create an online shop with that same aesthetic. He would be the first shop in his hometown to serve this aesthetic. Julian now had to pick up some competencies related to being an online shop owner. He learnt about web design. He learnt about digital marketing. He learnt about supply chains. He learnt about e-commerce. He set up his online shop, and created various social media accounts to drive sales and marketing. It started off slow, because, obviously, no one had heard of him yet, but he persevered. He reached out to some known influencers in his town who were putting out content on Instagram and got them to give him a shout-out. He contacted some kids who had a large following on TikTok and sent them some cutesy hats, bags and dresses for review. "Now I can be loli like a lollipop. LOL!", quipped one kid on his TikTok video. Julian's shop was gaining traction. He, too, was getting attention. He was contacted over email by a high school newsletter wanting to know about the man behind the fashion. Julian knew it was now time to retell his story. Should he hide his old brand of being a clothing manufacturing executive? Should he incorporate it into his new brand story? He decided to cleverly weave them together. During the interview, he told the high school newspaper the following: "I have always wanted to own an online shop. I find the cute aesthetic endearing and, to be honest, suitable for everyone. It's not just for kids. It's for the kid in you. In fact, my wife and daughter are both fans of the cute aesthetic. They've got all these cute plushies and figurines all over the house. They watch anime together too. As for me, I cut my teeth in the manufacturing industry where I was exposed to a great variety of clothing styles. I learnt how to develop new clothing products, and I learnt a whole lot about materials too. One day, I decided, hey, why not? Let's open an online clothing store specially dedicated to cute clothing and accessories. And you know what, once I got started, I never looked back."

As you can see, Julian never once thought of himself as an employee of a factory. He always saw himself as an industry professional in the clothing manufacturing industry. When the tide turned, Julian was resilient. He identified his options, assessed their feasibility and responded to the changing times.

The Benefits of Personal Branding

He created his own opportunities. He knew that his shop could not and should not compete based on price. How could he? Giants like Shein would simply overshadow him with their insanely low prices, huge selection and free shipping. He knew he had to compete based on target market differentiation. And to target that market, he needed a persona for his shop. A cutesy one, to serve those who are fans of cutesy clothing and accessories. He also knew he needed to pick up new knowledge and new skills, with a good attitude. Not just by using a template, though. He needed to know his stuff inside out. Julian also knew that he eventually would have to retell his story. People would want to know where the man and the brand came from, and how dedicated they would be to this new space.

Sending a clear signal to the market and industry

And so you've gained a competitive advantage over your fellow professionals. You're keeping the momentum of the industry by staying relevant. You're continually aware not to let the private side of you adversely affect the professional side of you. You've trained yourself to be resilient to the shocks of the industry. But what good is all that? Well, all that sends a clear message to the market and industry about what you stand for as a professional.

You see, the market is full of "noise". There are a lot of people talking at the same time. There are many professionals making claims to having made great achievements, many professionals looking for jobs and a whole host of other noises. "I've just won an award for top researcher in the string theory field," says one over LinkedIn. "Belated birthday gift from my boss!

Thank you, boss!" says another over Instagram, accompanied by a carousel of photos of that gift. "Dinner with colleagues," says yet another over Facebook, accompanied with a wefie. This is all noise that says a lot while saying nothing at all. You need to cut through the mix and send a clear signal to the market and industry. And a personal brand helps you do just that.

How so? Well, the persona helps you connect to a similar personality in the market and industry. As a professional, you will be wearing this persona like a heart on a sleeve. The persona is backed up by its muscle, competencies. The market can see the knowledge, skills and attitude that you bring along with you. And the story helps to make your personal brand memorable.

Now, the market is not a monolithic space. It is segmented, and sometimes even fragmented. Only businesses without brands can treat the market as monolithic, because they're going for mass appeal with their products. But anytime a brand is involved, both for companies as well as for professionals, the market will appear as segmented. This is why, in branding, we always conceptualise "target markets". If we are going for mass appeal, then there would not be a need for a "target", would there? Now, when we conceptualise target markets, we always conceptualise a "primary", "secondary" and "tertiary" market. A primary market is the market that we want to target most. We will spend the most time, money and effort targeting that market. Typically, this market will be the one that shares the same personality as our brand. And this market will in turn choose us because what's important to us is also important to them. People who cut their hair at Supercuts will always go back

The Benefits of Personal Branding

to Supercuts, and people who cut their hair at neighbourhood barber shops will always go back to the barber shop, right? The secondary market is always the second choice to us. It does not exactly share the same personalities as us, but even with the differences, our business or professional relationships will still be functional. We will spend time, money and effort targeting this market, but a little bit less, since it's just not our first choice. The tertiary market is the one that we're not going to really bother with. This is because there is too great a difference between their personalities and ours. We know that there is a chance that this market may be attracted to us, but since they and our personalities are too different, we are not going to spend time, money and effort on them. If they wish to do business with us, we will oblige, but we're not too hung up even if they don't want to do business with us.

Now let's see how this applies to personal branding. Jennifer is a professional in the creative industries. She's great in videography, photography and animation, employing innovative camera angles, shot sizes and composition techniques to really make her products pop. She's a little bit irreverent, a little bit quirky and a little bit experimental, but everyone knows she gets the job done at the end of the day. Jennifer is looking for a new job and puts herself out there in the market. She sends her resume out to recruitment agencies and updates her LinkedIn accordingly. She formats her resume and LinkedIn using words that clearly show her professional persona. She uses a layout in her resume and a banner in LinkedIn that aesthetically fit the "anti-design" art style as a visual identity of her professional persona. She gets a call from three companies and decides to give them all a go. She meets with the people from the first company and sees that they too are rather quirky. They dress in saturated colours and have office decorations that juxtapose seemingly unmatched art styles, but she knows that it was done intentionally. They're rather informal with each other in the office, and curse words flow like water. "These people are quite like me," she thinks to herself. "I might like this company a lot." She meets with the people from the second company and sees that while they're informal, they're not exactly quirky. They do wear jeans to work and have drinks every Friday, but their office decorations were really thought out to fit a singular art style. "OK," she thinks to herself. "These folks are OK. They may not be a whole lot like me, but I think we can make it work." Jennifer pays a visit to the third company. These folks are very different from the first two. They seem more formal. Although they have empathetic policies like a "blue skies policy" every Friday and work-from-home arrangements, these are strictly regulated by protocol. While Jennifer respects where they're coming from, she doesn't think she would fit in very well with that company. They, too, may not enjoy working with her. Her professional persona and the company's personality just have a very awkward fit. Unsurprisingly, Jennifer decides to sign with the first company. Had the second company offered her instead, she would have taken the job too. But if the third company had offered her a job, she would have had to think long and hard about taking up their offer. She would have taken it if she really needed the money, but if she had a choice, she wouldn't have.

Taking stock

I really suggest you start thinking about your personal brand, if you haven't already begun. Any effort you make towards your personal brand will be worth your while. Remember, you BYOB. You build your own brand.

The more you work on building your personal brand, the more you work towards gaining a competitive advantage over other fellow professionals. You will be working towards creating value for yourself, where you are able to carve out a niche without much interference from other competitors. You will also be working towards establishing a sense of uniqueness about your persona, competencies and story. Having value and rarity would mean that you, as a personal brand, would be difficult to imitate. All that is left would then be for you to organise yourself to take control of the opportunities that present themselves to you.

The more your work on building your personal brand, the more relevant you will be in the market and industry. When you start off your personal branding project, you may not be aware of the diversity of competition from fellow professionals in the market. You may not be aware of the competencies that are needed. You may not possess those competencies yet. But that's OK. The more you work on it, the more aware you will become. The more you learn, the more you know. The more you practise, the better skills you will have. The more you apply this knowledge, the more mastery you will gain over the subject matter.

The more you work on building your personal brand, the more cognizant you will be of your image. The more vested you are in your personal brand, the more important your image becomes to you. You will become more and more particular about maintaining that image because of the time, money and effort you have put into building that image. The risk of "the many watching the many" is a risk that will always be there, and will become even more transparent as we move into Web 3.0. I had an inquiry once from a client as to whether she could funnel her OnlyFans account to her OpenSea account, and subsequently sell her OnlyFans content as NFTs. I told her that the funnel could be easily set up with an omni-channel strategy, but she had to be aware that any and all transactions that she made on her OpenSea account could be viewed on Etherscan. So, if she was concerned about being discreet (as many OnlyFans content creators are, for obvious reasons), she would do well to understand that Web 3.0 is far less discreet than Web 2.0.

The more you work on building your personal brand, the more resilient you will be in the event of any shocks to the system. By having your eyes on the industry at all times, you will be aware of complementary competencies that can be developed. You will know how to reach out and develop these competencies so that the shock to the system does not affect you too greatly. Only with a strong personal brand will you be motivated to keep your eyes on the industry. One who is too lulled by the comforts of their company and industry will be less motivated to pay attention.

The more you work on building your personal brand, the clearer your signal will be to the market and industry. Your main objective is to establish a clear signal amidst all the noise. In music production, we call this "cutting through the mix".

The Benefits of Personal Branding

Instruments which play in the same harmonic range tend to get muddled. Their individual timbres tend to blend into each other such that it becomes difficult to discern one from the other. Guitars and keyboards tend to play in the same harmonic range, as do bass guitars and kickdrums. What do music producers do? They alter the harmonics so that each instrument's timbre becomes more distinct from each other, thereby, "cutting through the mix". The most important aspect of sending this clear signal through is so that you reach your primary target market. Appealing to your primary target market is important both for them as well as for you. Because they share the same personality as your brand persona, they would enjoy working with you. And conversely, you would enjoy working with them. In the off-chance that you decide to work with your tertiary target market, the working relationship would be rather transactional. There wouldn't be much joy on both sides, with the relationship being kept for instrumental reasons.

I hope that this chapter has convinced you that you should start working on your personal brand. In the next chapter, I will look at *when* you should start working on your personal brand. It is never too late to start, but you should also bear in mind that branding is a continuous process. Along the way, you might need to refresh your brand to adapt to minor changes in the market and industry. You may also need to rebrand as a response to more serious changes.

CHAPTER 4

The "When"

Once, during an interview with a well-known university in the Philippines, I was asked what I would tell my 20-year-old self. Without hesitation, I replied, "I would tell myself to start developing a personal brand, and always keep my eye on it."

As an advocate and practitioner of personal branding, I highly recommend you start as early as possible. As soon as you enter the workforce as a professional, your branding should start. As the concepts and examples in earlier chapters serve to illuminate, no one expects you to keep that brand forever. Even the oldest, most traditional of company brands, such as Kongo Gumi (Japan, operating for 1,400 years), Stiftskeller St. Peter (Austria, operating for 803 years) and Staffelter Hof (Germany, operating for 862 years) have not stuck to the same branding. They have refreshed their brands and rebranded many times over the years.

The "When"

Some of you may have heard the term "ABC: Always Be Closing". This term is a popular mantra used by salespersons referring to how a salesperson should always be in the mindset of closing deals, using whatever tactics are necessary. This phrase originated from the 1992 movie *Glengarry Glen Ross*, starring Alec Baldwin. Now, while this phrase is appealing for the cash flow, for the purposes of our personal brand, we must also remember to ABB, "Always Be Branding". Always Be Branding refers to how we, as professionals, must always take stock of how our brand is positioned in the market and industry. We must always be custodians of our brand. We must always be aware of the value that our brand brings to others. This is known as "brand equity". A strong personal brand has a high brand equity, and a high brand equity brings about the benefits we have seen in the previous chapter. With a high brand equity, we will be able to gain a competitive advantage through our value, rarity, inimitability and organisation, stay relevant, mitigate the risks of "the many watching the many", build resilience and send a clear signal to the market and industry.

Look at the case of Josaiah. Josaiah did his Bachelor's in the liberal arts. Josaiah didn't know what he wanted to do with his career beyond graduation. He never really gave it much thought. When he graduated, he saw several job ads for government jobs. He knew that his Bachelor's degree was a rather general one, and so were government jobs. Most of these jobs weren't directly related to what he studied in college. Josaiah decided to give it a go anyway. He applied to these jobs and landed one fairly quickly. Josaiah has been in the government service for a while

Rebrand Yourself, Retell Your Story

now. Josaiah has never had a personal brand. He primarily identifies himself as a "career administrator". Josaiah is happy and comfortable where he is now, but as we have seen in the previous chapter, there could be a variety of conditional and event risks that could disrupt his position, and he might be left out in the cold.

Compare that to the case of Jesse. Jesse did his Bachelor's degree in IT, majoring in information systems. His college required a six-month internship as a requirement for graduation, so Jesse was assigned to work with one of the internship host companies that had registered with his college. Jesse thought that it would be with a large IT firm where he would learn more about the practical workings of information systems, but to his dismay, he was sent to work for an F&B company that sold cookies in mall kiosks. Jesse decided to carry on with it nonetheless, noting to himself that he wasn't in any position to make any demands yet with his limited experience. Jesse staffed one of these mall kiosks and quickly noticed how the inventories in the kiosk didn't actually tally with the inventories back at the warehouse. That was going to be a problem not just for the supply, but also for accounting and point-of-sales. He wondered if the other kiosks faced the same issue. Jesse noted how he had to inform customers that a certain flavour was out of stock, and yet receive a shipment of that very flavour later on in the day. Jesse knew there was an opportunity in this somewhere. At the next staff meeting, Jesse raised this issue to management. He asked if there has been an issue with excess stock and low sales. The finance manager, sales manager and warehouse manager

The "When"

looked at each other and nodded. Jesse suggested that it might be due to the stock management systems that didn't "talk" to each other. The warehouse used one platform, the kiosk point-of-sale used a different platform, and the accounting team used yet another platform. Jesse informed them that he was about to graduate with a degree in information systems, and that he could help them set up an application program interface that would allow these three systems to talk to each other. There would be no loss in communication, and the three departments could work on bigger and better things instead of worrying about excess stock and low sales. The general manager thought it was mighty intuitive of Jesse to identify this potential solution, and took Jesse out of kiosk sales and asked him to build them an application program interface. Jesse was happy that he was asked to contribute, but more importantly for our purposes, Jesse's personal brand was thus born. He became "the business systems guy for F&B".

Now, Jesse's personal brand does not and should not stop there. It should not be cast in stone for the rest of his economically active life. His personal brand, as well as all of ours, should be refreshed from time to time. He, just like us, may need to rebrand at a certain point as well.

In order to conceptualise brand refresh and rebranding exercises, we turn once more to the risk management framework. Earlier, we looked to the risk management framework and learnt about conditional and event risks. For every type of risk, be it conditional or event, there will always be some parameters that we can use to assess the risk. Firstly, almost every risk has an early-warning indicator, with the exception of black swans and dragon kings. Black swans and dragon kings appear out of nowhere, which is why we refer to them alternatively as "emergent risks". Early-warning indicators are signals that the risk is about to happen. Early-warning indicators always appear before "triggers", which are the points in time in which risks happen. For our personal brand refresh and rebranding exercises, we should be paying attention to developments in the industry and the market. In doing so, we are looking out for early-warning indicators. We should undertake our brand refresh or rebranding exercises when these early-warning indicators happen. We should not wait for the trigger, because it would be too late then. If we hear, for example, that there is a new legal requirement for certification in our profession, we should take action as soon as the law is passed. That is our early-warning indicator. We should not wait for the trigger to happen, for example, when being uncertified would cause us to lose a chance at employment or lose our ability to practise.

Aside from early-warning indicators, we should also pay attention to two other parameters, namely, probability and impact. Probability is a gauge of how likely a certain risk would affect us. We should note that not all risks would affect everyone equally. Different professionals with different expertise, experience and organisational support might be affected differently. You should assess the probability specifically for your own position in the industry. Do you have enough leverage to reduce the probability? An industry professional with a limited skillset, for

The "When"

example, might have a higher probability of being affected by the risk factor. Another industry professional with that same skillset, along with other complementary skillsets, might have lower probability of being affected. Yet another professional, whose position in his company of employment gives him protection from the changes in the wider industry might also have a lower probability of being affected.

Accompanying probability is the parameter of impact. Impact is a gauge of how much damage the risk might do, assuming that it manifests. Would it cause minimal damage to our personal brands, or would it affect our personal brands critically? Would it just be a teardrop to the sea, or would it be a tsunami that sweeps us away? Risks that require us to pick up a complementary skill, for example, have a minor impact on our personal brands. Even without picking it up, we can still get by in the industry. There are still tons of baby boomers who are still economically active, yet are not competent in working with computers. They are still able to get by by delegating the task of computer work to younger or more junior colleagues. Risks that might derail us, on the other hand, include risks such as a huge shift in the market and industry away from our professions. For example, the demand for jingle composers has diminished greatly with the shift away from television and radio advertising to digital marketing. I mean, be honest, when was the last time you heard a jingle in a social media advertisement? Prior to Web 2.0, we'd hear jingles multiple times a day on the radio and on the television. Jingle composers have had to pivot away to do other things. In other words, they have had to rebrand.

Both probability and impact considered, the greatest urgency for us to take action is for a risk that has a high probability of affecting us and would have the greatest impact on our personal brands. Factoring in early-warning indicators and triggers from earlier, our action should take its cue from early-warning indicators instead of waiting for triggers to happen. The formula for us to take action would thus be:

$$u(A) = v(EWA) + P + I$$

where

u(A): urgency of action to mitigate risk
v(EWA): visibility of early-warning indicator(s)
P: probability of risk occurring
I: severity of impact

Unfortunately, as humans, we tend to ignore early-warning indicators. In our rationally irrational minds, we tend to only take action when the trigger is visible (we can see, smell, touch, taste or hear it) and proximal (close to us) because we think that the probability is increased when the trigger is visible and proximal. Otherwise, we tend to think that "that's not going to happen to me". Just how many people ignored the call to wash their hands regularly and wear masks until they themselves were infected with Covid-19?

The "When"

Brand refresh

So when should we refresh our brand? Now, it is important to remember that industries change. Job requirements change. Job roles change. Customer requirements change. When these changes are minor and don't affect how the market and industry see us, all we need to do is update ourselves with these changes. When these changes are minor but throw us a little off-road, we should refresh our brand. We refresh our brand so that it remains relevant in the industry, and is responsive to the new changes to the industry, job requirements, job roles and customer requirements. In reference to the risk framework above, we should refresh our brand when we notice the early-warning indicator, when the probability is high but the impact is low.

Consider the case of Joel. Joel has always loved music since he was young. He learnt to play a couple of instruments and wrote a couple of songs but he soon discovered that he was best at promoting talent. In high school, he would be the person to look for if you wanted your demo tape to be played on the school radio. He was the one to see if you wanted your band to be mentioned in the school newsletter. Joel loved meeting new bands and listening to their music. He loved working on their album art and their flyers. He loved cornering the school deejays and editors and hounding them until they agreed to make mention of the bands he was promoting. When Joel graduated from college years later, he decided to establish an indie label. He was going to do most of the artiste and repertoire (A&R) work, and he'd get a couple of other people to help him out in design, marketing and promotion. He is proud to say that more than a couple of the artistes he promoted made their way onto the local radio stations. He felt fulfilled when he saw their CDs in shop windows across town. In the 2000s, music consumption patterns changed. With the release of the iPod in 2001, the Microsoft Zune in 2006 and the Creative Zen in 2007, people lost interest in CD players. People were still buying CDs for the most part, but only to "rip" them and share the tracks in MP3 format. That required Joel to change tactics. CDs weren't going to be the key to an artiste's success anymore, so Joel decided that he would refresh his brand. He was still going to keep up his A&R work, but he wasn't going to brand himself as "the guy who can get you played on radio" anymore. He was going to be "the guy who can get your merchandise in stores". He was going to shift his focus from getting airplay and producing CDs to producing merchandise and getting live performances for the artistes under his management. The way he saw it, the music was going to make its rounds around the internet for free anyway, so it was going to be a free promotion for him. What was key now was fandom, and what do fans want? To see artistes perform live and to buy merchandise. Joel noted how this was a different revenue model than in the past. In the past, he would recruit "street teams" to distribute flyers, stickers and demo CDs around town. Not anymore. Now he needed to be the toughest negotiator for concert venues and merchandise manufacturing deals. The industry changed again in the mid-2010s. Streaming services gained in popularity. Musicians uploaded their own content to YouTube, Instagram and Facebook. TikTok allowed for open sharing of sound clips to be

The "When"

made into videos. Live performances and merchandise just didn't cut it anymore. What did Joel do? He refreshed his brand once again. He now became "the guy who could get musicians followers on social media". With the monetisation potential of social media, Joel capitalised on that for his personal brand. Today, Joel helps musicians get their music listed on Spotify, sets up subscriptions on Patreon and Ko-Fi and promotes livestreams on TikTok, where musicians can get donations directly from their fans.

As you can see, a brand refresh responds to the minor changes in an industry. It doesn't take much to do a brand refresh. The professional only has to have a keen eye in identifying these minor changes and respond accordingly. Brand refreshes generally still maintain the personal brand, but with an update to suit the current tastes.

Rebranding

A rebrand, on the other hand, is a more significant set of actions that is caused by more significant reasons. We should engage in a rebrand when our current brand is losing, or has lost its effectiveness in efficiently engaging with the market and industry. Conditional and event risks may have affected the ability of our brand to perform as it used to in the past. In reference to the risk framework above, we should rebrand when we notice the early-warning indicator happening, when the probability is high and the impact is high. Situations that might require a rebrand would include:

- Josephine is finding it harder and harder to get clients for her business these days. Seems that not many people are asking for such services anymore.
- Justin lost his job because many companies in his industry moved their production facilities overseas.
- Jade discovered that she can't get by with the skills she learnt back in college anymore. There are completely new skills she has to pick up.
- Jeremy got into fisticuffs with some stranger one night at the bar. He was charged with disorderly conduct. His company decided his actions didn't suit their image, and he was let go.

A rebrand requires the professional to recreate his brand persona, obtain new competencies and retell his story. It's a major transformation that the professional must go through in order to retain his relevance as an industry professional. It also requires him to make a very important decision regarding his former personal brand. He must decide whether to incorporate it into his new brand, to retire the former brand completely, or to keep the former brand in hibernation until such a time when it can come back to life.

Consider the following scenarios:

Josephine is finding it harder and harder to get clients for her business these days. Seems that not many people are asking for such services anymore. It is to be expected. There are many platforms these days that can perform the tasks that she and her fellow professionals used to do. Mobile apps, desktop apps,

The "When"

cloud-based web-apps, you name it. Some of these apps even have an artificial intelligence engine that makes the work performance more powerful the more people use it. She knew she could not compete with them. She decided to do a self-brainstorm to see what related skills she could offer instead. She found one that she really liked. And it wasn't going to be a huge uphill battle picking up this skill, since it was already related to the skill she currently has. Josephine went ahead and signed up for an online course. She would learn the formal knowledge of this skill from this course. She also read a lot of blogs on the topic, and watched a lot of YouTube videos so that she could get a sense of the tacit information regarding this skillset. Josephine put her knowledge to practice, building a portfolio along the way. When she was satisfied with her level of competency, Josephine offered this service to her clients. Her new brand story incorporated her former brand. She sold herself like this: "Coming from a background in desktop publishing, Josephine upgraded her skills to the new millennium. Desktop publishing provided her with the necessary design skills that would seamlessly transit into her new love: UI/UX design. She built her skills in UI/UX design by applying her expertise in print design to the digital space, specifically for websites, mobile apps and webapps. She is a firm believer in strong foundations. Without solid ground underneath your feet, you can jump as high as you want."

    Justin lost his job because many companies in his industry moved their production facilities overseas. It wasn't just him, of course. His fellow professionals, too, were now jobless due to this shift. Justin had two choices. He could either move to another city, where other companies in the same industry were located, or rebrand. He listed down the pros and cons of both options. The first option would allow him to continue being a professional in the same industry, but it would be a ticking time-bomb. The movement of his company to an overseas facility was an early-warning indicator and it would be a matter of time before the trigger points hit other cities too. After all, everyone in the industry knows that labour and rent are cheaper overseas. The second option would require a lot more work on his part but would ensure better stability. Justin decided to bite the bullet and go for the second option. He got wind of new job roles which were in demand due to their emphasis on digital processes and products. Recognising the importance of the digital space in the digital era, Justin felt it was a way forward. But this was very different from what he used to do. He would need to take time off to really study the subject matter. Justin enrolled in classes at the local community college. The entire program lasted for three months, and Justin really gave it his all, determined to rebrand. At the end of the program, Justin looked for a job in that new industry with his new personal brand. The initial reaction Justin faced was that he was much older than the other applicants. The hiring managers were suspicious as to whether Justin could perform as well as the other applicants. After all, it was widely known that older people tended to be less digitally savvy. Justin got the feeling that his age might be against him, so he decided to build a portfolio. He offered to build digital products for his friends based on what he learnt at the community

The "When"

college. He popped all these products into an online portfolio and demonstrated them at every interview moving forward. Knowing that his former personal brand had not even a tangential bearing on his new personal brand, Justin kept the former brand in the freezer. It wasn't something he was ashamed of, so he wasn't going to retire it completely. He was also hopeful that one day he might be able to thaw it out again. After all, he did work hard on his former personal brand. He now sells himself this way: "With humble beginnings in the automotive industry, Justin found himself at a crossroads and took the digital road. He is proud to call this his second wind, and is determined to make the digital world his forever home. Justin is still learning about this ever-evolving digital space, but is confident that he has amassed significant knowledge and experience to command his own little ship in this wide digital ocean."

    Jade discovered that she couldn't get by with the skills she learnt back in college anymore. There were completely new skills she had to pick up. Unfortunately, the company she worked for was not very forward-looking, and was operating in a rather outdated manner. Not content to be lulled by the comforts of the company, Jade spent her evenings and weekends updating herself on the changes in the industry. While she initially thought that these changes were minor, Jade soon discovered otherwise. She had to learn new computing languages, calculus and new ways of presenting the final product. It was lucky that she had a strong base though. Otherwise, picking up these new skills would be even more challenging. She saw her new personal brand as an extension of her former one. As such, she incorporated both together. This is how she describes herself now: "With a solid foundation in statistics and probability, Jade is now a Machine Learning specialist, or as she likes to call it, the statistician of the digital season. Jade is not only skilled in data analysis; she is also able to build scripts that allow data to build upon itself and analyse itself. She now works with Supervised Learning models of big data, especially in the areas of recommendation engines and remarketing campaigns in order to generate actionable insights that will have a positive effect on meeting returns on investment".

Jeremy got into fisticuffs with some stranger one night at the bar. He was charged with disorderly conduct. His company decided his actions didn't suit their image, and he was let go. Jeremy found it difficult to find another job in the same industry, because people talk and the industry is small. Jeremy decided to rebrand himself. He decided on what he wanted to do next, chose a different persona, picked up some new competencies and worked on retelling his story. Jeremy didn't want any link between his past and his present. He regretted his moment of weakness, and also was not particularly happy about how his company let him go instead of backing him up after all the talk about being a "family". Jeremy decided to retire his old brand completely. He never made mention of his former personal brand ever again, and worked on promoting his new brand. When asked about his working experience, Jeremy cleverly downplayed his old brand in his story. He would say: "Coming from a background in advertising, I decided to venture out into the world of financial services. After all, financial services is no

The "When"

different from advertising. Financial services require me to promote my product and to educate the client on how this product can be meaningful to them. It is not formally a form of advertising, but it is advertising nonetheless. Without knowing all the features and functions of the product, and how they can use these effectively, clients may not be aware of the power of the product in helping them."

So when should we incorporate our former brand into our new brand? We should consider doing so only if our former brand can flow smoothly into and can add value to our new brand. Ask yourself: Will your new brand be enhanced by incorporating the former brand into your brand story? Will the audience see a link between your new brand and your former brand?

Julius was formerly a chef. He wanted to try something new so he signed up for the police academy. He cannot find a way to show how his choice to become a law enforcement officer is linked to his former profession. He can't show how being a chef enhances his knowledge of law enforcement. Julius should not incorporate his former brand into his new brand.

Jessica was previously doing work in full stack web development. She became attracted to the Web 3.0 space and picked up some competencies in NFT marketing. She became well-equipped with airdropping, using bots on Discord servers and influencer marketing. She took on her new personal brand as an NFT marketer. She could make sense of how her background in web development helped her in her new brand. Her experience in Web 1.0 was a natural evolution into her involvement in Web 2.0, and subsequently in Web 3.0. Her participation in the "open source" culture of app development allowed her to seamlessly accept the mindset of blockchain technology and the transparency of transactions that came with it. Her knowledge of Python allowed her to analyse and even write off-chain smart contracts. This association also came intuitively to the audience. The technological leanings of cryptocurrency and its subsequent manifestations such as NFTs and DeFi could be intuitively linked to Jessica's former brand, especially in their usage of common terminology such as "i/o" (input-output). Jessica would do well to incorporate her former brand into her new brand story.

When should we retire our former brand completely? We should retire our former brand completely if the former brand is going to negatively affect our current brand. There are many instances when the former brand can affect our current brand. Most of these reasons revolve around the audience's perception of the former brand. These perceptions can be quite societally specific, so I shall only give one scenario below:

John used to be a professor. The university circuit wasn't working out for him. Although he was actively publishing and teaching, he didn't see a future in it. He decided to leave. He tried looking for jobs with his qualifications, but alas, all the responses he got were that he either was "overqualified" or "lacked experience". It was very disappointing for John, because he saw great value in what he had been doing, but he couldn't change the market perception. He really did not have any experience outside of the university circuit, which meant that potential employers could not give him anything but an entry-level position. And entry-level positions didn't require a PhD. Plus,

The "When"

potential employers were not willing to match his last-drawn salary, not for an entry-level position at least. Plus, they were worried that the entry-level job might not be mentally stimulating enough for him, which might cause him to want to leave. That was definitely a concern for potential employers because they didn't want to spend time and resources training someone just for them to leave soon after. Needless to say, John had a lot of difficulty getting a new job. He even tried to return his PhD to the conferring university, thinking that without it, his life would be less encumbered by it. That was a no go. The conferring university didn't want to take it back, but did suggest to him not to declare it in job applications. After much trial and error, John ended up with some new competencies that would soon become his new personal brand. John decided to retire his former personal brand. He was happy with his new personal brand, and didn't want the former one to affect his new personal brand. His former brand was thus tucked away, never to be heard of again.

When should we keep the former brand in hibernation? We should keep our former brands in hibernation when we cannot as yet make sense of how to use it in our new personal brands but we know that it might come in handy in the future. This would be the best option for the majority of professionals. The former brand can be thawed out at any time and incorporated into the new personal brand when the situation permits.

Jimmy did his degree in theatre studies. At first he did want to become a thespian, but seeing as how difficult it was to break into that industry, he soon decided a career change was in order. After all, he wasn't keen on being seen as a "starving artist". Jimmy took on some writing gigs and found that he was quite talented in that area too. He took up some short courses on creative writing and found a job at a local newspaper. He did pretty well for himself, and championed his writing as his personal brand. His former personal brand in theatre was still there, but it was put into hibernation. After all, he had no use for it as a writer. "Waste not, want not," thought Jimmy. Time passed by, and Jimmy soon found himself writing for company blogs and social media posts, known generically as "content writing". One day, Jimmy encountered a new trend in content writing. The word "storytelling" was being thrown around as a method of engaging the audience and reducing the "bounce rate" on company blogs. "Beautiful," thought Jimmy. "I can bring my theatre brand out again." After all, storytelling was something that was ubiquitously taught in the theatre studies program, and leveraging on that aspect, he could market himself so much better as a content writer.

So how do we make sense of our former personal brands in relation to our new personal brands? And what of our hobbies? Some of us have developed our hobbies into such great passions that we develop competencies in that area. Noobs have even asked our help to introduce them to the basics of the hobby. Isn't that our personal brand as well? Or part of it? How do we make sense of all these?

In a more meta perspective, the professional must conceptualise himself as the brand custodian of a "house of brands" instead of a "branded house". A branded house is a model (or some say "architecture") of branding where there are many

The "When"

sub-brands under the parent brand, but all of the sub-brands are marketed and operated under the umbrella of the parent brand. Sub-brands are not allowed to dominate each other, or to overshadow the parent brand. They all must exist cohesively under the parent brand. Google, for example, has Google Drive, Google Calendar, Gmail and many other sub-brands under its care. In fact, the only (known) sub-brand that does not fall under the Google umbrella is Google's Magenta project, which aims to use machine learning as a tool to make music and art. One could say that the branded house concept is a "centralised" model of brand building. It's like a fortress, and all the sub-brands work in unison like different divisions of the fortress militia. The fortress stands strong and tall because of its command of the divisions of its militia. But once a siege is successfully laid upon the fortress, it all comes down crumbling like a house of cards. That's unfortunately the biggest downside to keeping one's brand in a branded house.

A house of brands, on the other hand, is a parent brand that is home to various sub-brands. All these sub-brands have their own separate operations and marketing. They maintain their own brand image separately from one another. Chinese tech giant ByteDance is a prime example of a house of brands. Under this parent brand, you have Douyin and TikTok (short-video sharing platforms), Toutiao (a content discovery platform), Xigua and Capcut (mobile video editing apps), Helo (a multilingual social media platform), Lark (an enterprise software) and BytePlus (a big data analytics software). The duty of the parent brand is to promote certain sub-brands as flagship brands, and to relegate other sub-brands as side brands. Flagship brands would be most strongly associated with the parent brand, while side brands would be distanced from the parent brand and the flagship brand.

You, as a human being, are the parent brand. You have a professional side and a private side. Unless circumstances allow, your professional side and your private side should not mix. Your professional side should be promoted as your flagship brand, while your private side should be a side brand. In the event that you decide to put your former personal brand into hibernation, it will also join your private side as a side brand.

This understanding of flagship brands versus side brands has been put to good use by many people in the Web 3.0 space as of late. Many of them have began declaring their flagship brands on their social media handles, especially on Twitter. Thus, we get handles like @Jojo.eth, which suggests to the audience that Jojo wants to be known as a professional focused on the Ethereum block chain. We also get handles like @Joni.sql and @Jaze.js, suggesting that these professionals are developers working with the SQL and JavaScript languages respectively.

Consider the following scenario regarding the private side as a side brand.

Justin is a compliance professional in the aerospace industry. As a compliance professional, Justin knows all the ins and outs of the legal conditions set for safety, finance and manpower in the aerospace industry. He carries with him a lot of tacit knowledge about the industry too, and he knows that people being people, will always try to bend the rules in their favour. He

The "When"

doesn't resent them for this. It's just human nature. But knowing this, he also knows that he can't be too friendly, because his job requires him to make others toe the line. If he were to be too friendly, they wouldn't take him too seriously. And if they don't take him seriously, he cannot get his job done. And there can be serious repercussions for poor compliance in this industry. Accidents can happen when people don't comply. Justin does not come across as a dictator, but he does command a certain respect. People in the industry know that they need his watchful eyes and ears "to save them from themselves", in the words of an aircraft engineer. This is Justin's personal brand. And this is the brand that he promotes as his flagship brand. "Without that brand," says Justin, "I am just another employee". Now, in his private life, Justin is deeply involved in Japanese popular culture. In fact, he is one of the leading artists in fan art. Fan art is art drawn about characters that exist in anime, manga or Japanese games. Some of this art can be, as we say, "not safe for work" (NSFW). Justin is happy to participate in this hobby. Yet, he never makes this hobby known among his colleagues in the industry. He never posts anything about this hobby on his LinkedIn page or shares any links related to this hobby with his colleagues. He distances this side brand from his flagship brand because they are as strange as bedfellows can get. There is a probability that his side brand might negatively affect his flagship brand, and so he does not want them to be seen in the same space together. Granted there are some colleagues who know. They found his hobby out by accident, spotting some photos of him at anime conventions. But even so, he still will not bring his side brand to stand out in the sun. "If I ever find a way to monetise this hobby, I will then make this my new personal brand," says Justin. "Until then, it remains underground where it is safe."

Taking stock

In this chapter, I have strongly suggested that you begin crafting your personal brand as soon as you can. It is never too late to start, if you haven't. You will gain a ton of benefits, as shown in the previous chapter.

Once you've more or less settled on a personal brand, you will need to keep an eye on the market and industry. That personal brand will not be your first and neither will it be your last. You must keep a lookout for smaller changes in the market and industry for which you would need to refresh your brand, or larger changes which would require a rebrand. Upon rebranding, we should decide what to do with our former brand. We can incorporate it into our new personal brand, if it can flow easily and add value into our new brands. We can retire it completely if we feel that it is going to hold our new personal brand back. Or we could just put it into hibernation until we can decide what to do with it.

As we continue this process, we may go through a good number of brands. We may also have developed our hobbies into something that might look like a personal brand. We then must conceptualise ourselves as a house of brands. We, as the professional, are the house, and we have many brands living in that house. We must decide which personal brand to push as our

The "When"

flagship brand, and which brand(s) to relegate to a side brand. We will be primarily known as our flagship brand, and we, in our professional lives, must keep a distance with our side brand. This is so that our side brand does not affect our flagship brand negatively. Tim Henson, who has been running The Distorted View Show (an adult-oriented comedy podcast) for two decades now is well known for having done this. Tim had been experimenting with comedy podcasting since Web 1.0. He did have a flagship brand as an accountant, and kept a full-time job in that role. He kept his podcasting as a side brand during that time. Around 2004, Tim discovered that he could and wanted to make podcasting his flagship brand. He began to take steps to push this side brand into the limelight by releasing episodes more frequently, and creating a subscription revenue model in order to realise this vision. Today, The Distorted View Show has a presence on the major podcasting platforms, as well as social media. It has worked with many sponsors and has plans to expand to other products beyond podcasting.

CHAPTER 5

Step 1: Developing Competencies

Now, we have taken a look at what personal branding is in the second chapter. We have taken a look at the benefits of personal branding, or why you should create your own personal brand in the third chapter. We have also taken a look at when you should start developing a brand, and when you should refresh your brand or even rebrand in the fourth chapter. In this chapter, and the next few chapters, we are going to take a look at the step-by-step recommendations that I have for you in (re)branding yourself and subsequently (re)telling your brand story.

Beyond that, you should work towards optimising your personal brand. Remember that your personal brand should be complete, but the personal branding exercise is never completed (doesn't that remind you of the old 7-11 slogan, "Always

Step 1: Developing Competencies

close but never closed"?). There will always be ways for you to optimise your personal brand to make it work better for you.

In crafting your personal brand, I recommend beginning with competencies. This is mainly because competencies without a persona is better than a persona without competencies. As mentioned earlier, a persona allows you to talk the talk, but competencies allow you to walk the walk. Armed with competencies but without an accompanying persona is acceptable. You will still be seen as a skilled person, just like other skilled persons. You can then take your time to fine-tune your persona in order to distinguish yourself from other professionals. However, having a persona with no accompanying competencies is a poor idea. Without the requisite competencies, your professionalism will be called into question. If you are unable to perform as expected of your persona, your reputation may be at stake. In the capitalist, industrial, modern societies in which we live, we are valued according to what we can give in relation to what we will take. It may not always be fair, but it is how our societies were built. Let's take a look at the following scenarios.

Jane is trained in digital illustration. She is a bit of a quiet character and not too fond of attracting attention to herself. In fact, one could quite easily say that she's quite the "plain Jane". The idea of having a personal brand persona is alien to her. She's as quiet in private as she is professionally. But she's good at her job. She takes on projects for any company that needs illustrations done for branding, packaging or marketing purposes. She has no preference for artistic style. Jane will survive as a professional.

Joanna sells herself as a digital illustrator. She claims to specialise in pop surrealism. She promotes herself as a "Creator", and claims that she regularly comes up with innovative digital art pieces that are "ahead of their time". Joanna is very confident in herself and carries herself very well. She landed a job in a book publishing company as a book cover illustrator. For her first task, she was asked to illustrate a pop psychology book that talked about one's inner demons. Confident, Joanna got to work. Her boss observed that she seemed not to know the standard illustration process of going from ideation to conceptualisation to prototyping to iteration. He waited to see what she came up with. To his dismay, her cover layout was problematic. She had the cover title in a single font type and font size spread across the illustration of a leaf. He was puzzled. What does a leaf have to do with inner demons, he wonders. And her typographic choice of a single font type and size baffled him too. "Where is the visual hierarchy?" he asked her. She replied, "Well, this cover design is going against all conventions, just like our inner demons." Frustrated, he replied, "Even in anti-design, there still must be design principles applied. I expected you to know that." Needless to say, her boss's confidence in her competency was shaken.

Now, even if you do possess competencies, it sometimes is not enough for the market and industry. Competencies are related to each other. Some competencies build upon each other in terms of difficulty level, while others build upon each other laterally in complementarity.

In other words, one may be competent in a certain subject

Step 1: Developing Competencies

matter, but over time, more difficult tasks may be required as a buildup upon the initial competency. One might be required to develop the skills to work on something more complex. One might start off as a Python programmer, but one might be called on to create supervised learning models in the future, and unsupervised learning models beyond that, such as in the case of OpenAI and Midjourney.

Or, one could be called upon to develop the associated management skills in order to manage tasks in that subject matter, or to develop the associated teaching skills in order to train others in the subject matter, or to develop competencies in subject matters proximal to the initial one. Decades ago, project managers managed projects armed with only their management skills. That equipped them with the skill of initiating projects, planning the deliverables, timeline, costing and risk responses, executing projects, monitoring and reporting completion statuses and closing projects. But many of them didn't have subject matter expertise in the subject area. The project manager for server architecture projects, for example, wasn't necessarily trained in server architecture. The project manager for fashion design projects too wasn't necessarily a fashion designer. This was a flaw in job design that needed to be overcome. Project managers who weren't trained in the subject matter weren't able to accurately predict scope creep. They weren't able to accurately predict the time and/or effort needed for certain tasks (waterfall project management measures time needed for tasks to be performed, while agile project management measures effort needed). They weren't able to procure new resources or redeploy existing resources should the project scope change while the project was in motion. They weren't able to successfully negotiate time, cost and quality when project scopes changed mid-way. Eventually, companies decided that they would engage project managers who not only had management skills, but also subject matter expertise.

A similar situation happened to instructional designers. Decades ago, instructional designers were instructional designers. They were adept at sequencing curriculum, writing learning objectives (both "enabling" and "terminal"), chunking and scaffolding learning content, and assessing learning. Many of them were proud to have instructional design as their one and only subject matter expertise. But there was also a design flaw here. Instructional designers were designing instruction for other subject matters. And they didn't have subject matter expertise in those fields. They weren't able to see the intricacies of each field and how different fields required different designs for instruction. Eventually, companies who were paying for instructional design services preferred to engage subject matter experts in specific fields, who also had instructional design expertise. That made a whole lot more sense for the workflow and final product.

The point is, having the requisite competencies should take precedence in your personal branding. It is the foundation of all personal brands, and one should always be cognizant to put the competency foot forward. So how do we begin developing competencies?

We will go through seven steps together. First, I would like you to identify your strengths, weaknesses, opportunities and

Step 1: Developing Competencies

threats. We will be using the familiar SWOT framework in business studies for this purpose. Then, I would like you to analyse the trends in the market and industry. We will be adapting the BCG Matrix, another popular tool in business, to our needs in personal branding. Thirdly, I would like you to empathise with yourself. No one can feel what you feel better than you. No one can think what you think better than you. We will use three tools from user experience research to get you to know yourself. Fourthly, I would like you to be honest with yourself and identify your performance gap. No, no, you're not that good yet. Neither are you that bad at all. There is a realistic performance gap that you must identify. Fifthly, you will then go onto the next step of "learning". I put forth some sequencing structures derived from the discipline of instructional design for your consideration. Sixthly, you will have to "practise". We will adapt the familiar Bloom's Taxonomy to this part. And finally, you will have to apply what you learnt and practised. The ultimate aim for you in this part is to build a portfolio that is relevant to the competency you developed and that you would be proud to show the world.

Step 1.1: Identify your strengths, weaknesses, opportunities and threats

Strengths, weaknesses, opportunities and threats is a popular business tool, acronymised as "SWOT". It enables you to see your current position in the market and industry, as well as how you can move forward in that industry. Ask yourself the following questions:

Question 1: What are my strengths?

Why are you asking yourself this question? Because you want to leverage on your strengths. That is to say, you should develop competencies based on your strengths. Leveraging on your strengths means that you would have a base from which to develop your competencies. You also might have some background knowledge and transferable skills which would be highly advantageous to you. I will explain why you shouldn't develop competencies based on your weaker areas in just a while.

I recommend that in listing down your strengths, you don't limit yourself to just one. Do a self-brainstorm and come up with as many strengths as you can. Don't worry about being accurate or coming up with a strength that others would be in awe of. No one needs to see this list but you. List out anything you can in any order you can, no matter how large, small or ridiculous. You may end up with a list like this:

- Working with people
- Marketing
- Getting a good rest
- Ignoring annoying people
- Making sense of chaotic situations
- Keeping cacti alive

Question 2: What are my weaknesses?

Why are you asking yourself this question? Because you want to avoid developing competencies in areas you are weak in. You won't have much of a base to develop those competencies upon.

Step 1: Developing Competencies

Furthermore, you don't have a whole lot of background knowledge or transferable skills between your weaker areas and the competencies you are going to develop. You will have an uphill battle. If I was weak in, say, mathematics, should I go ahead and try to develop a competency in data science? No, because I have to first overcome my weakness in mathematics, before I even start on data science. Otherwise, I would seriously suffer in the sections of data science that concern statistics and probability.

Now, I'm not preventing you from working on your weaknesses. You are most welcome to. When we work on our weaknesses, we become stronger as a person. But please work on your weaknesses separately from developing competencies. It is hard enough to work on weaknesses, and it is equally hard to develop competencies. It is infinitely more difficult to work on them together at the same time. Imagine a situation where a person is bad at sports. Sure, he should work on this weakness and try to improve his strength, endurance and hand-eye coordination. But imagine him, already being bad at sports, trying to go pro. The learning curve would be too much for him to bear. He would be not only trying to scale himself up, but he would be trying to scale himself up to a professional level of competency in an area where he is weak in. I recommend that in listing down your weaknesses, you don't limit yourself to just one. Do a self-brainstorm and come up with as many as you can. Don't worry about being accurate or hiding your true weaknesses from others. No one needs to see this list but you. List out anything you can, in any order you can, no matter how large, small or ridiculous. You may end up with a list like this:

- Math
- Theory
- Memory
- I'm too naive
- Working independently
- Staying out of trouble

Question 3: What are the opportunities available to me as an industry professional?

As an industry professional, none of us are at a dead end. There is always a way, if we look hard enough for the opportunities. Some opportunities present themselves. Some opportunities, we have to create. Opportunities present ways for us to move forward as an industry professional.

I recommend that in listing down your opportunities, you don't limit yourself to just one. Do a self-brainstorm and come up with as many opportunities as you can. Don't worry about how feasible those opportunities are. No one needs to see this list but you. List out anything you can, in any order you can, no matter how large, small or ridiculous. You may end up with a list like this:

- Get a job in an MNC
- Offer to do pro bono work
- Network far and wide
- Update LinkedIn regularly
- Become an influencer
- Start a small business

Step 1: Developing Competencies

Question 4: What are the threats to my position in the market and industry?

In any environment, there will always be threats. In the animal kingdom, the only animal safe from threat is the apex predator, and even then, he's there for the taking when he grows weak and old. The younger apex predator is going to have a go at his throne. As a professional, we must recognise that. There are, and will always be, threats around.

Now, I know it is always good to be positive and all. It's good to have a rosy view of life. But ask yourself, by being positive, are you being realistic? I mean, I could always have a positive view of humanity and cross the street without looking, since I know behind every vehicle sits a very nice driver who will avoid hitting me, right? I could always also step into a den of hungry lions knowing the power of positivity would save me too, right? Wrong.

I recommend that in listing down your threats, you don't limit yourself to just one. Do a self-brainstorm and come up with as many threats as you can. Don't worry about being accurate or being politically correct. No one needs to see this list but you. List out anything you can, in any order you can, no matter how large, small or ridiculous. You may end up with a list like this:

- Automation
- Artificial Intelligence
- Social justice warriors
- My age
- My gender

In answering these four questions, you may find the template provided below helpful.

Within yourself	
Strengths	*Weaknesses*
Opportunities	*Threats*
External to you	

Now that you've SWOT-ed yourself, what do you see? You might see that:

You have some strengths, which you can leverage on. Your strengths are your core muscles. Over time, you might build stronger core muscles or perhaps more muscles, but what's on your list now are what you can use. You will also discover that sometimes, your strengths coincide with your interests. At other times, though, you may be strong in something that doesn't

Step 1: Developing Competencies

interest you. You might be great in sales, although you dislike doing sales. You might be good at mentoring others, although you really don't see yourself as a mentoring type.

You have some weaknesses which you are aware of. Of course, you will also have strengths and weaknesses that you are not aware of. They're not on the list, duh, because you don't know of their existence. In due time, they might reveal themselves. The important thing to know about weaknesses is that you should indeed work on them. Weaknesses are internal threats, and the one thing you should not do is let threats turn into real issues that will impact you. Just as is the case with your strengths, you will discover that sometimes you are weak in things which disinterest you, but at other times, you are weak in things which interest you. You might absolutely be smitten by audio production, but you're just weak in it. For the life of you, you can't figure out why your mixes sound so "mid-dish" (which the lay person would describe as "dull") but when other audio producers emphasise the mid tones, their mixes still sound pleasant. Now, it is easiest to work on weaknesses which you have interest in. You will be motivated to work on them, as compared to weaknesses which you have no interest in. If you have no interest in sales, and are weak in sales, well then, you'll find it a chore to even work on that weakness. Every single cold call you make will be a dread, and you will exhale a sigh of relief when the call is over. But as mentioned above, do avoid building your competencies for your personal brand upon your weaknesses. It will be an uphill battle.

Thirdly, you might see that there will be opportunities

available to you if you look for them hard enough. Some opportunities present themselves to you, while others you can create for yourself. Being invited to join a professional organisation, or being headhunted for a job are opportunities that present themselves to you. In this digital age, creating opportunities for oneself is easier than ever. Gone are the days of the hierarchical organisation monopolising professional opportunities, as was the case during the Industrial Age and Technological Age. In the 1970s, "new institutional" economists theorised that there were two organisational patterns, namely, the "hierarchy" (persons employed with a "Contract of Service") and the "network" (persons engaged in a "Contract for Service"). These days, the decentralisation of professional opportunities allows us to create opportunities for ourselves. Networking, for example, is one example of creating opportunities for ourselves. Participating in several gig economies is another. Offering work pro bono in order to build our chops is yet another. There are accordingly various digital platforms that we can leverage to create opportunities for ourselves. Social media and video sharing platforms have allowed many people to monetise their skills as content creators and consequently, become thought leaders in their areas of expertise. Rick Beato and Adam Neely, for example, have created "video essay" content discussing music theory in depth. Max Maher has done the same for the crypto space, and Tom Nash for the financial markets. Beyond that, there are also opportunities on instructional platforms for those who wish to teach via asynchronous e-learning. There are also opportunities on project platforms for gig economy work.

Step 1: Developing Competencies

Fourthly, you might see that there will be threats to your professional life. Your professional life neither exists in a vacuum nor is set in stone upon graduating from college. As we moved from Web 1.0 to Web 2.0, one key word that has always been on the lips of organisations is "disruption". Many organisations, especially tech organisations that see themselves as "unicorns", are on a mission to become the apex predator in their product area by disrupting the business status quo. Thus, we saw Facebook (now known as Meta) completely disrupting the social media space that was previously dominated by Friendster and MySpace. And Facebook right now is trying to hold on to its youth. As I mentioned earlier, the apex predator too grows old, and new predators will vie for its apex position. Now, what do we do with threats? First of all, we do not let them become issues. When threats manifest as issues, it will have an impact on us, which we then would have to deal with. And how do we not let them become issues? Well, taking reference to the risk management framework we learnt about earlier, we can either avoid them by giving them a wide berth, transfer them to another person to take care of them for us, or by buffering ourselves so as to reduce their impact (if and when they manifest). Sometimes, though, we might have to just accept these threats and live with them. Say, for example, you feel threatened by artificial intelligence. Indeed, there are people out there who genuinely feel that artificial intelligence will take over their professions and even their private lives. What can you do about this? You could choose to completely avoid artificial intelligence by going into an industry where artificial intelligence will not reach (such as mining and agriculture). Or you could choose to transfer the threat of artificial intelligence by banding with other professionals who know how to deal with it. Or you could choose to reduce its impact by developing competencies that are complementary to machine learning (in this instance, the cliche, "Keep your friends close, and enemies even closer", does apply quite well).

So what do you do with these insights on your strengths, weaknesses, opportunities and threats? Hang on. Let's hold that thought until we get to the next step, and then we'll be able to use these insights in a more actionable manner.

Step 1.2: Analyse market needs and industry trends

Every country has an economy, and every economy has industries and every industry has a market attached to it. In a capitalist system, where there is private ownership of assets, land, equipment, resources and inventory, the market drives the industry, and the industries drive the economy. The demand comes from the market, and the industries provide the supply of what their markets need. Australia, for example, maintains a skilled occupations list for migrants to fill the dearth of supply for professions that their markets need.

Therefore, in order for us to choose competencies which we want to invest time, money and effort in developing, we need to identify what the market needs, and what the industry trends in response to market needs are.

But why? Can we not just choose to develop competencies in areas of our interest? Yes, we can, but it would not be wise to do so. The reason is that all skillsets are equal, but some are

Step 1: Developing Competencies

more equal than others. There are skillsets which are high in demand (from the market) and high in supply (from the industry). There are skillsets which are high in demand but low in supply (as in the case of Australia above). There are skillsets which are low in demand and low in supply. There are skillsets which are low in demand and high in supply.

We can refer to the popular BCG Matrix to make sense of the four permutations above. The BCG Matrix measures the potential growth of a product area with reference to two axes, namely, the market share of the product in relation to competitors and the market growth rate. Products with a high relative market share and a high market growth rate are termed as "stars" because they potentially can generate high amounts of revenue (but beware, they also need high capital outlays). Products with a low relative market share and a high market growth rate are termed as "cash cows" because they potentially can generate high amounts of revenue with low amounts of capital investment. Products with a low relative market share and a low market growth rate are termed as "dogs". These products don't make much money but at least they don't require high capital outlays. Products with a low relative market share and a high market growth rate are "question marks". These products don't make much money but require high capital investment.

Adapting the BCG Matrix to our purposes of developing competencies, we could thus say that:

- Skillsets which are high in demand and high in supply are cows. Many opportunities for your personal brand to get noticed and grow. Many professionals with the same skillset. Y'all will get your own li'l piece of heaven.

- Skillsets which are low in demand and high in supply are question marks. There are just too many professionals with that skillset for you to make an impact. Plus the market doesn't really need that skillset.
- Skillsets which are low in demand and low in supply are dogs. You can make an impact with your skillset in the industry because not many professionals possess that skillset, but your personal brand cannot grow because there aren't many opportunities in the market.
- Skillsets which are high in demand and low in supply are stars. You can make a huge impact with your skillset in the industry because not many professionals possess that skillset, and your personal brand can exploit many opportunities.

The next step for you is to go to job portals such as Glassdoor to find out skillsets which are currently being advertised for and the average salaries. Research as extensively as you can and identify skillsets which you are interested in. You could be interested in them because of the high pay, because of the status or simply because you have an intrinsic interest in the subject matter. Go ahead. I'll pause while you do this research.

You're back? Now it is time to pare down the skillsets step by step:

Step 1: Developing Competencies

- First, cut out the skillsets which coincide with your weaknesses.
- Second, cut out the skillsets which coincide with the threats you foresee.
- Third, cut out the skillsets which you do not have opportunities for. Perhaps these skillsets may be too expensive to pick up, such as medicine-related skillsets. Perhaps these skillsets may take too long to pick up, such as a difficult foreign language.

What you will be left with are skillsets which capitalise on your strengths and have available opportunities within reach. You will likely have a natural predisposition to, background knowledge of or transferable skills in those skillsets. You will also likely be in a good position to either exploit opportunities that present themselves to you, or to create your own opportunities in relation to that skillset.

Step 1.3: Empathise with yourself

Empathy is defined as putting yourself in someone else's shoes to see their points of view, pains and desired gains. Now, how about if you put yourself in your own shoes for a change?

The reason I say this is that more often than not, we are trying to fill someone else's shoes. We are trying to be someone that our significant others want us to be. Your romantic partner, your parents, your BFF all have an image of who you should be. But who do you want to be?

After the exercise in analysing market needs and industry

trends, you now have a selection of competencies that you could possibly develop. What you need to do now is to find out a little bit more about those skillsets. Text a friend. Google the information. Watch some YouTube videos.

Next, let's use some familiar tools in user experience research. Let's start with the "empathy map". Empathy maps are used in user experience research to better understand the users who we are designing user interfaces for. In this case, we are using it as a tool of introspection to assess what we found out and consequently how this information has influenced how we feel emotionally about certain skillsets and how we make logical and rational sense about certain skillsets.

Ask yourself the following questions:

- What did you find out about each skillset?
- What do you emotionally feel about each skillset?
- What do you rationally/logically think about each skillset?

This exercise will help you narrow down even further to a smaller number (or even just one) skillset that you wish to develop a competency in.

Following that, we will use these introspective insights to build a "user persona" for ourselves. The user persona is another tool in user experience research that is used to visualise the audience for whom we are designing. In this instance, we are using it to build something akin to a "vision board" for ourselves. In building our user persona, we should list down the following:

Step 1: Developing Competencies

- Motivations: Why do I want to adopt this skillset?
- Fears:
  » What am I afraid of for the journey ahead?
  » What can I do to allay those fears?
- Desired gains (incorporating another user experience tool, the "MosCow Method"):
  » Must have
  » Should have
  » Could have
  » Won't have

You may wish to use the following template for this exercise:

Results of my initial research		
My feelings		
My thoughts		
My motivations	*My fears*	**Desired Gains**
		Must have
	My response to fears	*Should have*
		Could have
		Won't have

What you might discover after doing this exercise is the following:

- Motivations: This will serve as a reminder to you throughout your competency development journey. You might even discover more motivations as you go along. Keep this in view throughout the entire journey. As soon as you discover that the motivations are gone, you will need to restart the empathy process. Why? Because motivations are your fuel. When the fuel is gone, and you can't top it up anymore, you might need to switch to another vehicle that uses a different type of fuel.
- Fears:
    » Your fears will likely mirror the threats you ideated earlier as part of the SWOT process.
    » Your tactics to allay those fears will serve as your risk responses. As mentioned earlier, whenever there is a threat, we can either avoid the threat, transfer the threat, reduce the impact of the threat, or accept the threat and live with it. The situation that most people will encounter is that they are torn between developing a competency that is of their intrinsic interest but has ambiguous returns potential, on the one hand, and developing competency in a subject matter that they don't have great interest in but has a huge potential return on investment. A person might have great

Step 1: Developing Competencies

interest in the hospitality industry but knows that it doesn't pay great. This same person may have no interest in the financial industry but knows that there are more benefits to be reaped. If that should happen to you, my recommendation is for you to try either competency first, give it a "trial period" and reevaluate your feelings towards it. This is because the answer to the dilemma between intrinsic interest and returns on investment is at best a Schrodinger's cat. If we invest "all in" on developing competencies that we are intrinsically interested in, we might regret the lower returns in the future. On the other hand, if we begrudgingly take up a competency we're not too interested in, sometimes we might develop an interest in it along the way; other times, though, we might grow to hate it even more.

- Desired gains:
  » Must have: This will serve as your main goal/objective in developing this competency.
  » Should have: This will serve as your secondary goal/objective in developing this competency.
  » Could have: This will serve as your tertiary goal/objective in developing this competency.
  » Won't have: These will serve as situations you wish to avoid after developing this competency. These include things such as, but not limited to:
    › Realising that there is low demand for this competency

> Realising that the development of this competency has taken more time, money and effort than expected
> Realising that you learnt the wrong things, which couldn't hold up in the real world

Step 1.4: Identify performance gap

The next step for you would be to identify your performance gap. In regard to the subject matter in question:

1. What do you know now?
2. What should you know by the end of the learning phase?
3. What are you able to perform now?
4. What should you be able to perform in order to meet your primary goal/objective?

This set of questions is the standard set of questions that instructional designers ask whenever they are doing a "training needs analysis" for learners.

How do you find out the answers to these questions? First of all, you would need to list down all the resources that you can find on the subject matter. Be as exhaustive as possible. Look through all possible avenues, including, but not limited to:

- Information on Wikipedia
- Content on YouTube
- Blog content searchable through Google
- Instructional videos on Udemy, Coursera and the like

Step 1: Developing Competencies

- Ebooks through Amazon, Scribd and the like
- Podcast episodes through Spotify, Audible and the like
- Courses offered by educational institutions

Secondly, you would then go through the descriptions or synopses of these resources to pick out keywords which jump out at you. Write all these keywords down.

Thirdly, you would then sieve out these keywords into nouns and verbs. The nouns will serve as the knowledge that you need to learn, and the keywords would serve as the abilities that you need to perform.

Now, try to map out your performance gap. You may wish to use the template below.

The Now	The Future
Current knowledge	What I need to know (the nouns)
Current abilities	What I need to be able to do (the verbs)

Step 1.5: Learn

Let's get ready to learn. In this phase, you are going to be concentrating on the "knowledge", that is to say, the nouns that you have distilled from the previous exercise. There will be some opportunities to practise your abilities (the verbs), but the emphasis should be on the knowledge first.

Now, in the prior step, you have already identified many resources that you could use to start learning. We shall now make use of these resources effectively and in an engaging manner based on your learning preferences.

The basic categorisation of learning styles in instructional design is that learners learn either visually, auditorily, kinesthetically or in a tactile manner. In my opinion, however, these learning styles matter most in classroom-based instruction. With the multitude of options available in the digital age, I prefer to use other categorisations that I have observed after many years working in instructional design.

I have observed that some learners prefer to learn through structured instruction, while others prefer self-directed learning. Structured instruction is where learning is structured according to a set curriculum and is directly taught either by an instructor or the proxy of an instructor, such as video. This is more of a top-down approach to learning where the instructor delivers the instruction downwards to learners. Self-directed learning, on the other hand, is when the learner drives his own learning without the help of one single instructor. The learner will try to make sense of all the resources he has on hand by making use of his pre-existing knowledge to connect to new

Step 1: Developing Competencies

knowledge, and subsequently, to connect all new knowledge together. If I want to learn graphic design, for example, I could always sign up for a suite of courses that teach me design theory, design thinking, colour theory, typography and the like. Or, I could alternatively watch a video on graphic design essentials, note down the keywords that I encounter such as "colour saturation", "organic shapes" and "golden spiral layout" and then go on to find out more about each keyword through other resources.

I have also observed that some learners prefer to learn in a step-by-step sequencing, while others prefer a whole-to-part sequencing. A step-by-step sequencing is where the learner wants to see the final product of his learning and then learns each step to reach the final product. These learners prefer to work with templates, checklists and clear signposts so that they may know where they are in relation to the final product. These learners also tend to be averse to theories and concepts, preferring to see the learning content as technical, practical information.

A whole-to-part sequencing, on the other hand, is where the learner wants to see the bigger picture (ideas, theories and concepts) first, and then learn the components that make up the bigger picture. They will try to make sense of how the components parts can be used in different permutations in order to come up with a final product of learning that fits the guidelines of the bigger picture. If I were to teach photo imaging, for example, I could show learners a composite photo that will serve as the final product and take them through each step, such as firstly, using "content-aware fill", then masking the layer, then adding a base layer, then matching the colour temperatures of both layers and so on until we reach the final product. Alternatively, I could present the objectives of photo imaging, and then show each tool that can be used, such as the lasso tool, the transform tool, the adjustment tool, the opacity slider, and so on.

Coincidentally, I have also observed that most, but not all, learners who prefer a structured instruction also tend to prefer step-by-step sequencing, while learners who prefer self-directed learning also tend to prefer whole-to-part sequencing.

Now, which style is yours?

If you prefer structured instruction and/or step-by-step sequencing, I recommend that you learn the subject matter of your choice through online instructional videos or by taking up courses in an educational institution. Do note, though, to not be lulled by the idea that a course can teach you everything you need to know about the subject matter. Subject matters don't work like that in the digital age. They are always related to either a higher level of difficulty, or to complementary subject matters. You should be cognizant that there will always be other courses that you can take to level up.

If you prefer self-directed learning and/or whole-to-part sequencing, I recommend that you follow a methodology of learning in the digital age known as "branching". This method allows you to build a fertile knowledge tree by making sense of the various pieces of information that reveal themselves as you uncover them through your learning. This method was popularised by early adopters of Wikipedia who would go through its pages by reading a page of their interest and then clicking

Step 1: Developing Competencies

on a link on that page that would take them to a complementary or related page, repeating that process on the page they landed on next. What I recommend you do is the following:

1. Choose any resource randomly.
2. Learn from it.
    » If you find the content and instructional delivery suitable, carry on.
    » If you find the content too difficult, bookmark it and go to another one.
    » If you find that you already know the content, skip it and go to another one.
3. Take notes by relating your pre-existing knowledge to that new knowledge.
4. Create a "parking lot" for new terms, concepts and theories that you encounter in this resource but missed out on while you were identifying your performance gaps earlier.
5. Repeat Steps 1 to 4. Delete items from the parking lot when they are explained and elaborated upon.
6. Stop when all the subsequent resources you encounter repeat what you already know.

It is now time to move to the next step, where you will work on the abilities (the verbs).

Step 1.6: Practise

Now, take out your list of verbs. Arrange the verbs in the order recommended by Bloom's Taxonomy, a popular tool in instructional design. In Bloom's Taxonomy, there are six levels of proficiency in performing a skill. These levels are structured from the easiest to the most difficult.

- Level 1: Remember. At this level, you just need to retain knowledge.
- Level 2: Understand. At this level, you should be able to summarise the knowledge you retained.
- Level 3: Apply. At this level, you should be able to confidently express your possession of this knowledge to others.
- Level 4: Analyse. At this level, you should be able to break down or deconstruct this knowledge into its component parts or steps.
- Level 5: Evaluate. At this level, you should be able to critique or appraise this knowledge that you possess. Which parts or steps do you agree with? Which do you think is not so agreeable?
- Level 6: Create. At this level, you should be able to produce a product as evidence of your learning.

Now, what we are going to do is work in the reverse order of Bloom's Taxonomy for this current exercise. That is to say, you are going to try creating a product as evidence of your learning (Level 6). And in that process, you should be able to:

Step 1: Developing Competencies

- Evaluate which parts or steps you agree and disagree with (Level 5)
- Analyse the requirements of the product as evidence by breaking it down into its component part or steps (Level 4)
- Revise what you've learnt about this subject matter (Level 3)
- Summarise the knowledge you obtained (Level 2)
- Remember the important steps and parts of the subject matter (Level 1)

You need to practise as much as you possibly can. I cannot say this enough. Practice may not always make perfect, but it will certainly make you faster, more confident and more able to tackle the next step.

Step 1.7: Apply

In this step of the process of developing competency, your terminal objective will be to build a portfolio that you are confident of showing to the public.

What is a portfolio? A portfolio is a collection of works that you performed for professional purposes. These works represent your personal brand. They do not have to be performed for commercial intent specifically, but they must be as high-fidelity a prototype as possible to what you will bring to the market. Your portfolio can be demonstrated in many ways, including but not limited to:

- Websites (mostly used by industry professionals who focus on management skills and/or services)
- Social media (mostly used by industry professionals who focus on physical and/or digital products)
- Platforms that support text display for code, markup and prose (mostly used by industry professionals who focus on programming)
- HTML5 publishing platforms (mostly used by industry professionals who focus on writing)

So how do you start building this portfolio?

- Level 1 (easy mode): *You have unlimited lives and can keep respawning from the same spot.* Find a suitable benchmark that you aspire to. Or find a role model you aspire to be like. Keep practising until you reach that level. The good thing about the easy mode is that you will hardly be disheartened. You will just continue practising until you reach the level you want to reach. When you're reached that level, you can create your portfolio and share with the world the results of your application. Now, the bad thing about the easy mode is that it's not reflective. You can't see what others see about you. What you think of yourself may not be that accurate, you see. My advice is that you should only go on easy mode if you really, really lack confidence. Otherwise, please consider the other modes below.

Step 1: Developing Competencies

- Level 2 (normal mode): *You have limited lives and can only respawn from a designated start point.* Show the products you created during the practice step. Get feedback. Iterate and improve on your products based on the feedback. The good thing about the normal mode is that you will get real feedback from real people. You will be able to see how people see your abilities. The bad thing is that if you don't improve, those same people will soon lose interest in giving you feedback. They might think that the time and effort they put in to analysing your products and giving you honest feedback have not been put to good use.
- Level 3 (hard mode): *Big mistakes = game over.* Offer pro bono services to anyone who is interested. Start with your immediate network of friends and family. Then go to friends of friends. This allows you to expand your network while also working on real-world tasks. But real-world tasks do come with real-world consequences. The pressure will be on, so watch closely the time you take to deliver and the quality of your delivery. People might seriously lose trust in your abilities should you make any big mistakes or repeat your mistakes. If you're the kind who works best under pressure, I recommend you go on this mode. The hard mode is the best way for you to develop mastery fast. You will need to make decisions on the fly, adjust and adapt quickly and figure out what works and what doesn't.

Rebrand Yourself, Retell Your Story

Whichever mode you choose, the final step for you would be to create your portfolio. First, you would need to choose where you want to upload your work. The four options listed above serve as a guide. You may choose whichever platform you like, or you may decide to go for other platforms too. In terms of interface, social media would be the easiest to upload to, but please don't upload to your private profile. Create a separate professional (or "business") profile for your portfolio. If you decide to upload your portfolio to a website, but are deterred by the complexity of web design, go for Google Sites. It's the easiest website to create and you can figure it out in a matter of minutes.

Second, you should upload the best examples of your work. Not everything. Only the best examples. Also, you should not include works that are not related to the competencies that you are carrying at the moment. Remember when we discussed in the previous chapter about incorporating, retiring or hibernating your former personal brand? You should only include your older works if you are incorporating your former personal brand into your current one. If you're retiring or hibernating your former personal brand, don't include the work you did back then in your new portfolio.

Third, you should include photos of yourself working. Photos of you working include a certain indescribable human element in your portfolio. It cements the idea in the audience that the competencies that you demonstrate are really yours. It also shows you in a more social or situational setting, lending further credence that you can work with others and apply your skills in a real-world context. But no duckface selfies, please.

Step 1: Developing Competencies

Fourth, include information about prestigious or successful companies that you've worked with (if any). It really helps if the audience knows that you've done something with Meta or ByteDance or P&G, or any other big name. Be careful, though, about corporate sensitivities. Works for which you have signed a Non-Disclosure Agreement should not be included. Also, be careful not to dox others without their permission. A stealthy screen capture of a Zoom meeting with a big-name client won't sit well with them, especially if their faces and names are clearly shown in your screenshot. If you haven't worked with any prestigious or successful companies, don't worry. You don't need to fret over dropping names. Also, don't drop names that the audience won't recognise. "Website designed for Bob" is not only going to be ineffective, it's going to cheapen your brand.

Taking stock

So, what have we looked at in this chapter? We've looked at the first step in developing your personal brand, that is, to develop competencies. For some of you, you might be branding for the first time. For others, you might be rebranding. For others, you might be toying with the idea of refreshing your brand. Whatever it might be, this chapter has looked step-by-step at how you can develop your competencies.

Step 1: Identify your strengths, weaknesses, opportunities and threats. You need to be honest with yourself and identify your own strengths and weaknesses. These are internal to you, and no one else needs to know about your own introspection but you. So don't worry about others thinking you're tooting your own horn (there are some cultures where humility is so revered that any mention of one's own strengths may be interpreted as arrogance), or exposing your weaknesses to others. You also need to put on a realistic thinking hat and think of external threats and opportunities available to you. The opportunities, you are going to have to think hard about. It's all too easy to go into the fatalistic mental model and blindside ourselves to hidden paths. Don't do that. Think creatively about new paths that can either open up for us, or we can open up ourselves. The threats, you are going to want to mitigate. That is, you can either find a way to avoid them, transfer them to someone else, or reduce their impact. Danger lurks around every corner, and still waters run deep. Your threats can be a person, a situation, an event or any other thing that could negatively impact your position as an industry professional. Don't be afraid of others thinking that you're just being a Negative Nancy. Again, no one needs to see this introspection of yours but you.

Step 2: Analyse market needs and industry trends. Before you decide on which subject matter you want to master, you should understand that not all subject matters are equally valued in the market and by the industry. When there is a high demand for that skillset, and there are lots of professionals who have that skill, everyone will get a piece of the pie. It's not a big piece, but it's sufficient. When there is a low demand for that skillset but there are lots of professionals with that skillset, it's going to be an uphill battle to make something of yourself in that area. When there is low demand for that skillset and there's not that many professionals who possess that skillset, everyone can

Step 1: Developing Competencies

indeed get a piece of the pie but there's really no room to grow. Conceptually speaking, the best situation would be where the skillset is high in demand but low in supply. Those who posses that skillset can make an impact and experience abundant growth. In order to decide on which skillset you want to master, you would need to search on job portals. Look for skillsets which are popular as well as those which you have an intrinsic interest in. Then pare it down. Cut out those which coincide with your weaknesses. Cut out those which coincide with the threats you foresee in the previous step. Cut out those which you do not have opportunities for. What you will be left with are skillsets which capitalise on your strengths and for which there are available opportunities within reach.

Step 3: Empathise with yourself. So how do you feel about the skillsets that you're narrowed down to? Are you thinking logically about them? Do you have an emotional attachment to them? In this empathy phase, we need to understand ourselves. We need to see ourselves from our own point of view. Are you motivated to develop competency in this area? Is there anything you fear about embarking on this journey? What do you desire to gain from this investment of time, effort and/or money?

Step 4: Identify your performance gap. Right now, there is a body of knowledge that you are familiar with. Right now, there are some abilities you can perform. But where do you want to be? What does the industry and market expect you to know and perform? You are going to have to identify this gap and work on it. The knowledge gap, you will cover by learning. The performance gap, you will cover by practising.

Step 5: Learn. Know your learning preferences. Choose your learning resources. Gather as much knowledge as possible until you have internalised all that information. Keep your mind open for new knowledge at all times.

Step 6: Practise. You're going to have to practice all that knowledge that you've learnt and create something meaningful out of it. The more you practise, the better you will get at it. You will develop your own internal processes and make sense of how all that information comes together as a comprehensive, practical and applicable body of knowledge.

Step 7: Apply. What you've practised so far is only as good as it looks to you. Do you know how it would fare in the real world? Not yet. Not until you apply it, that is. Ultimately, your main objective in applying all that you've practised is to build a portfolio that you can be proud to show to the public. Once you've done that, you can safely say that you can walk the walk.

The next chapter will be about how you can craft your own brand persona. Again, you might be using this for your inaugural personal brand, or for a rebrand, or for a brand refresh. No matter what it might be, the competencies you worked so hard to develop now need a face, some sick threads and some pumped-up kicks. That's where the brand persona comes in.

CHAPTER 6

Step 2: Craft Your Brand Persona

A brand in the digital age is nothing without its persona. Sure, there were older brands which were established a long time ago that didn't quite bother about their persona upon inception. But do you realise that with the rise of social media in Web 2.0, most of them began to develop a brand persona? Brands like Adidas, Redwing and Dove now are championing their personas. They've personified themselves so that they may attract potential customers of the same personality.

As an industry professional, if you don't have a persona, you will be offering your competencies as-is. There will be no qualitative differentiation between you and the next professional. You will certainly be appreciated and compensated for your competencies, but then again, so will other professionals.

The persona helps you to distinguish yourself from other professionals while at the same time reminding the market and industry of your capabilities.

We will be going through six steps. The first step requires you to change your mindset. I will urge you to renounce the employee mindset because it keeps you in too comfortable a position within your organisation of employment. It also leaves you vulnerable to risks that creep up on you unawares, as well as risks that jump at you out of nowhere. As an industry professional, on the other hand, you will keep an eye out for changes in the industry. You will also learn to be resilient to bounce back from major shocks to the market and industry.

The second step requires you to depersonify yourself so that you will be lucid about your private side and your professional side. You are entitled to live as a private individual, but I highly recommend that you be careful that your private side does not negatively affect your professional side.

The third, fourth and fifth steps require you to repersonify yourself. You do so by first identifying a core archetype that is most often associated with your chosen profession. You then identify an influencer archetype that you are comfortable in carrying. Amalgamate the two, and now you have your own brand persona.

The sixth step requires you to work on your brand persona directly following the third, fourth and fifth steps. The sixth step will be broken down into eight sub-steps for the sake of clarity. Guidance will be given for you to create your brand name, brand slogan, brand voice, brand values and anti-values, brand

Step 2: Craft Your Brand Persona

visual identity, brand vision and brand mission. I will discuss how your brand name should be able to demonstrate your subject matter expertise while distinguishing yourself from other professionals. I will also discuss how to write your brand slogan, with examples. These exercises in brand name and brand slogan creation require a fair bit of ideation on your part. You will come up with some gems and some stinkers, that's for sure. But trust the process, and the perfect name and slogan will come along. The next few steps will flow smoother once you get your brand name and brand slogan right. You will then practise crafting a brand voice in formal, technical, casual and simple ways. I'm going to discuss which voices best fit which archetypes. Remember to maintain consistency. Your brand voice will speak on your behalf whenever you appear in publications or social media. I then will move on to brand values and anti-values. Brand values are what is expected of your chosen archetypes, and anti-values are just the opposite. As an industry professional you should keep within your brand limits by sticking to your chosen values, and avoid stepping into your anti-values territory. I then turn to your brand visual identity, which is how you present your brand visually to the public. This, too, should be consistent throughout the logo you use, the photographs you post and the banners you use, among others. Your last two sub-steps would be the brand vision and mission. The brand vision sets you upon a time horizon, where you forecast your goal of mastery. The brand mission is going to be the activities that you do. These activities will be strongly featured in your brand story.

Step 2.1: Renounce the employee mindset

You are not just an employee of an organisation. You are an industry professional. An employee of an organisation has the organisation as its ecological system. It gets its resources from there, and yes, it's quite a comfortable little environment. The organisational employee can be so comfortable that he doesn't even look out the window. He doesn't pay attention to what's going on outside because he doesn't have to. The resources his company provides keeps him satisfied. The employee carries around his name card as a badge of honour. He is happy for as long as the organisation has his back, but he does leave himself vulnerable in some ways.

An industry professional has the entire industry as its ecological system. The industry professional keeps one eye on the organisation and one eye out the window. He likes to observe and learn what's going on outside. Not to be unappreciative of the resources bestowed by the organisation, mind you. Just to be aware of the changes happening outside so that he may capitalise on opportunities and mitigate the threats that he sees happening in the industry. The industry professional carries around his personal brand. He sees the need to distinguish himself from other professionals. He wants to use his brand to gain competitive advantage. In order to do that, he will continually stay relevant to the industry. He will keep his eye on what the market needs and what other professionals in the industry are providing in response to the changing trends, and figure out a way to match the others. Because of that, the industry professional is one tough cookie. He trains himself to be resilient

Step 2: Craft Your Brand Persona

because resilience is the only trait that he can hold on to when going gets tough.

You are not just an employee of an organisation. You are an industry professional. Renounce the employee mindset.

Step 2.2: Depersonify yourself

You are a person. You are defined by your cognition, your construction of the world around you and your actions. You are complex. Even if you may think that you're a simple, happy-go-lucky, unassuming person, you are actually complex underneath that veneer of simplicity that you see yourself as.

Your cognition is how you make sense of stimuli from the world around you. You store this understanding in a part of your mind that is known as the "schema". Your earliest memories, the experiences that stand out and your most recent experiences enter your schema quite easily. (In psychology, these are technically known as the "primacy effect", the "Von Restorff effect" and the "recency effect" respectively.) Now, whatever information that resides in your schema will try to maintain your mental stability. It will tend to stay there, unchanging for as long as it can. Of course it will. If that information were to be in constant flux, you wouldn't be able to make sense of the world (and this is why people remember the rainbow as having seven discrete colours instead of being a blend of hues). Now, new stimuli from the environment will try its best to enter your schema. Stimuli which are agreeable to the information already residing in your schema will be admitted entry. They will serve as reinforcements of the information which is already in there.

Stimuli which go against the information already residing in your schema will not be easily admitted, not without a fight at least. If you encounter a piece of information that is antithetical to what you already know, you will tend to either reject it outright, or try to rationalise it. Whatever information remains in your schema will guide how you see the world. Until the next stimulus comes along.

Now, what happens when the way you see the world meets with your observations of how the other people around you behave? That's when your mind will start to construct meaning. Your mind will construct various meanings depending on how far your cognition is from the way others behave. If the way you behave is exactly similar to how others in society behave, your mind will be at ease. You will construct a very simple paradigm that you fit very well in this society. However, if the way you see the world is very different from the way others around you behave, you will experience what sociologist Robert Merton calls "anomie". It's a state of existential discomfort which needs to be resolved. Depending on your individual schema, you might decide to:

- Conform: You will convince yourself that society is right and that you should try as best as possible to understand, accept and follow how others behave.
- Innovation: You are not convinced that society is right and so will try to find innovative ways to skirt around the system so as not to get in trouble for the way you think.

Step 2: Craft Your Brand Persona

- Retreat: You are not convinced that society is right, but since you cannot win against it, you will just retreat into your own cosy corner where you can think the way you want to.
- Rebellion: You are not convinced that society is right, and will go against it head on.
- Ritualism: You will simply behave the way society wants you to behave while keeping your thoughts to yourself.

Now, I am not going to advise you to be a conformist, innovator, retreatist, rebel or ritualist. But what I am going to suggest to you is to depersonify yourself. That way, you mitigate the risk of your audience not agreeing with the way that you think as a private individual. Through the action of depersonification, we will distil our private selves from our professional selves, so that in the next steps, we can repersonify ourselves based on our professional selves.

Step 2.3: Identify a core archetype based on your area of competency

You will then need to identify a core archetype based on the subject matter that you developed competency in. Ask yourself: how do people in this profession generally behave? Their behaviours are proxies for how society expects them to behave, which is how you should conceptualise their archetypes.

Go through the list below and check off the archetype with the highest likelihood.

	Behaviour	Archetype
[ ]	Combative and rebellious against the norms	Outlaw
[ ]	Fantastical and mysterious	Magician
[ ]	Protective and strong	Hero
[ ]	Sensual and intimate	Lover
[ ]	Playful and humorous	Jester
[ ]	Polite and welcoming	Everyman
[ ]	Caring and empathetic	Caregiver
[ ]	Commanding and authoritative	Ruler
[ ]	Innovative and always with fresh ideas	Creator
[ ]	Unassuming and child-like	Innocent
[ ]	Wise and guiding	Sage
[ ]	Intrepid and bold	Explorer

I shall just give some examples to guide you along. In most societies, medical professionals fit the Caregiver archetype. In most societies, soldiers, firefighters and law enforcement fit the Hero archetype. You make the call as to what archetype best fits your chosen competency.

Step 2.4: Identify an influencer archetype that you are comfortable with carrying

It is okay to skip this step if you want to be seen as an industry professional just like any other. But if you want your professional brand to be noticeable and distinguishable, you should

Step 2: Craft Your Brand Persona

choose an influencer archetype that you are comfortable carrying. I advise you not to choose an influencer archetype that you are not comfortable with, as it will weigh down heavily on your personal brand as time goes by.

Are you comfortable acting in a sensual and intimate way with your audience (for example the way Marilyn Monroe did in her lifetime)? If not, the Lover archetype is not for you.

If you wish to brand yourself as an educator, are you more comfortable being all playful and humorous (like John Keating played by the late Robin Williams in *Dead Poets Society*)? Or are you more comfortable being commanding and authoritative (like Terence Fletcher played by J.K. Simmons in *Whiplash*)? Choose the archetype you are most comfortable carrying.

Step 2.5: Amalgamate your core and influencer archetypes

You now need to amalgamate your core and influencer archetypes. In the table above, two adjectives are given for each archetype. The simplest way to amalgamate is to now have four adjectives, that is, the combination of both archetypes. These four adjectives will now describe your brand personality. Let's see how two people might amalgamate their archetypes.

Jemma is intent on becoming a healthcare professional. Healthcare professionals are known to be Caregivers, but Jemma also wants to be a Sage. Her resultant brand personality is therefore "caring, empathetic, wise and guiding". Can you imagine her brand personality? She'd listen to your health problems and give you the best care possible. She will not be dismissive about your concerns, but instead give you thoughtful and wise solutions. If she were to be just a Caregiver, she would exercise care and empathy while attending to you. But she might not give you thoughtful and wise solutions.

Jolie is intent on becoming a cybersecurity specialist. Cybersecurity specialists (specifically white hatters) are known to be Heroes, but Jolie also wants to be a Caregiver. Her resultant brand personality is therefore "protective, strong, caring and empathetic". Can you imagine her brand personality? She'd keep a watchful eye over her clients' digital "properties" (to use the word popularised by Google Analytics) and shield them with encryption technology. She'd also try to understand why security issues occurred and patiently explain to clients how to avoid such security issues from recurring in the future. If she were to be only a Hero, she'd come in and save the day, for sure. But she wouldn't be giving you tips on how to prevent security issues from recurring.

Step 2.6: Build up the components of your brand persona

How is the market and industry going to recognise your brand personality? You can't keep mentioning all those four adjectives every time you meet a potential employer, client or collaborator, can you? Imagine Jolie shaking a dozen hands at the next cybersecurity conference and saying "Hi, I'm Jolie. I'm protective, strong, caring and empathetic". That would look ridiculous.

You need to craft the components of your brand persona

Step 2: Craft Your Brand Persona

which will communicate your brand personality clearly to the market and industry.

The components of the brand persona are your:

1. Brand name
2. Brand slogan
3. Brand voice
4. Brand values
5. Brand anti-values
6. Brand visual identity
7. Brand vision
8. Brand mission

Each of these components represents a different way of communicating the message of your brand to others. There are two general principles of creating the components of your brand persona:

1. Each component must be an expression of your amalgamated brand personality.
2. All components must tie in together seamlessly.

Step 2.6.1: Choose a brand name

For a personal brand, a brand name is the name that we wish others to know us by. It is an expression of our professional identity that speaks of our competencies while at the same time distinguishing ourselves from other professionals. It is not enough these days to be known by the regular name of our profession. Calling ourselves a "network engineer", "architect" or "music producer" no longer cuts it. There are already a lot of people who share that same title with us, and a lot more that lay empty claims to it. Every so often, we get people claiming to be a "wealth guru" or "crypto expert" or "influencer" or whatever other professional title without actually having the competencies to back it up. Social media is full of these types. The only true competency they have, honestly, is that they're great at making pitches.

So how do we come up with a brand name?

Step 2.6.1.1: Collate all the nouns used in and around the profession that we would like to brand ourselves in. These would comprise near-synonyms of the general professional category, nouns for the sub-specialisation, as well as nouns to describe the products. So let's say for example, we're interested in branding ourselves as a digital marketer. The words that would come up would be:

- PPC
- SEM
- SEO
- Black hat
- White hat
- Social media
- Guerrilla
- Online
- Digital
- ... and others

Step 2: Craft Your Brand Persona

Another example would be if we wanted to brand ourselves as a data scientist. The words that would come up would be:

- Big data
- Analytics
- Machine learning
- Artificial intelligence
- Neural network
- Algorithm
- Python
- ... and others

Step 2.6.1.2: Pick out nouns that we wish to be known for. Turn one of those nouns into a personal noun by adding "-er" or "-ist". Put those nouns together.

Putting together the nouns we collated for digital marketing, we might come up with the following combinations:

- White hat SEO algorithmist
- Digital guerrilla strategist
- PPC lead generator

Similarly, putting together the nouns we collated for data science, we might come up with the following combinations:

- Machine learning devops algorithmist
- Neural network analyst
- Artificial intelligentsia thought leader

Step 2.6.1.3: Pick a combination that rolls off the tongue. Oftentimes, whatever sounds nice usually has a rhythmic logic to it. There are many rhythms that our ears have been accustomed to. These include our normal speaking rhythm in English, which has been dubbed as the "Lombard rhythm" or "Scotch snaps", the dembow rhythm which has been used in much of Latin music these days, and the bossa clave, which is used a lot in bossa nova. Whenever we feel that something sounds nice, it is often because the emphasis on the syllables fall on the downbeat of these familiar rhythms. We don't really think about these things explicitly though, not unless we're trained in music theory and composition. We just feel that it sounds nice.

Step 2.6.1.4: Check against the archetype(s). Would your chosen archetype(s) use that brand name? Here again, we go with feel. There are no real technical dimensions to measure. Nonetheless, here is a guide to this step.

Archetype	Brand name should sound relatively...	Brand name should not sound too...
Outlaw	Combative and rebellious against the norms	Accommodating
Magician	Fantastical and mysterious	Stoic
Hero	Protective and strong	Weak
Lover	Sensual and intimate	Frigid
Jester	Playful and humorous	Serious
Everyman	Polite and welcoming	Elitist
Caregiver	Caring and empathetic	Cold

Step 2: Craft Your Brand Persona

Ruler	Commanding and authoritative	Meek
Creator	Innovative and always with fresh ideas	Common
Innocent	Unassuming and child-like	Bold
Sage	Wise and guiding	Youthful
Explorer	Intrepid and bold	Safe

Step 2.6.2: Create a brand slogan

The key to writing a good brand slogan is that it should be able to be used as a quote. Quotes can seamlessly enter any conversation, and once it does, there will be an automatic brand recall to the brand which uses that slogan. Nike's "Just do it" is a prime example. "Just do it" can easily be inserted into any conversation. For example, if you're conversing with a person who is unsure whether he should make a certain decision, you might say, "Come on, just do it!" By saying this, you would automatically recall Nike, who uses that slogan. Another example would be L'Oréal's "Because you're worth it". This can also be inserted into conversations such as a romantic conversation between a couple. Upon presenting the other person with a gift, the giver can always say "Because you're worth it" as a form of verbal reinforcement of the act of giving. And with that, L'Oréal's brand immediately comes to mind.

Now, there is indeed some controversy to this topic. American Express's former slogan, "Membership has its privileges", and Lucky Strike's former slogan, "It's toasted", have garnered significant attention in the branding world, with some saying that these slogans are not good because they're stating the obvious. Of course membership has its privileges. Why else would anyone be a member of anything if not for the privileges given, right? Of course it's toasted. All tobacco is toasted before being made into cigarettes. My professional opinion on this is that it doesn't matter if it's stating the obvious. What matters is that it rolls nicely enough off the tongue for it to be used in conversations.

Now, for a personal brand, your slogan is something that you're comfortable with calling your "catchphrase". It is also something that people will immediately associate with you. Whenever someone else uses words that resemble your slogan, they would say, "Hey, that sounds like something (insert your name) would say!"

Here are some examples of brand slogans that might inspire you:

- John Doe, Social Media Algorithm Optimiser: "You say twerk it, I say tweak it"
- Jane Doe, Sales Strategy Storyteller: "Always a happily ever after"
- Jack Doe, Interior Design Artist: "Building it like Bob, one brick at a time"

Step 2.6.3: Craft a brand voice

The brand voice is the tone of voice, composed of the lexicon and grammar of your personal brand. How do you start crafting your brand voice?

Step 2: Craft Your Brand Persona

Step 2.6.3.1: Try writing a paragraph. This should be a simple paragraph such as: "What I like most about [insert your profession of choice].

Let's see how that would look for the profession of graphic design. I am going to write in my most natural way first:

What I like most about graphic design is that it allows me to communicate visually with my audience. I get to translate what the client says in words into visuals for use by the client. I get to apply design principles and exercise my creativity.

Step 2.6.3.2: Rewrite that paragraph in a more formal way. There's always a more formal way to write something. Formal language is an umbrella term to refer to legalese, bureaucratic language, business language, the Queen's language, and many others. For our purposes, we will focus on business language, since it is the lexical and grammatical grounding for professionalism. Here's how I would rewrite my paragraph more formally:

What I appreciate most about graphic design is that it allows me to execute visual communication for the intended target market. Graphic designers are enabled to translate the product owner's words into visuals for branding and marketing purposes. Graphic designers will apply design principles effectively, efficiently and in an engaging manner.

Step 2.6.3.3: Rewrite that paragraph in a more technical way. Writing in a more technical way means that you're dropping more jargon in there. Here's how the above paragraph might look like, written in a more technical way:

What I like most about graphic design is that it allows me to express myself as a creative through the visual communication of illustrations, photoimaging and moving images. I get to interpret design briefs, ideate and prototype design ideas for my client. I get to apply visual hierarchy through the use of colour palettes, form design and typography.

Step 2.6.3.4: Rewrite that paragraph is a more casual way. Now, you could also write with more casual grammar. And of course, certain words have a more casual connotation than others. If I were to rewrite the paragraph above in a more casual manner, it might look something like this:

What I love most about graphic design is that I get to let my creative juices flow through graphics, pictures and videos. I get to say what the client means in my own special way through visuals. I get to work with the client to get the best possible result that everyone's happy with.

Step 2.6.3.5: Rewrite that paragraph in a simpler way. Sometimes, your audience may be more inclined to read something simpler. I once worked with a client that asked for revisions to the content I wrote for them. What was the issue? I used words like "heavyweight" and "gargantuan" to refer to industry thought leaders. They wanted words which were easier to understand by the common man. So how would I write the paragraph above in a simpler way? It might look like this:

What I like most about graphic design is that I get to draw and edit graphics, photos and videos. I get to work with the client to make a design that they want. I get to apply my skills and be creative.

Step 2.6.3.6: Check against the archetype(s). Of course, there are infinitely many other different ways to develop a brand

Step 2: Craft Your Brand Persona

voice. But for a personal brand, these four main types of voices are what you should be aiming for. Now, once you've done that, you need to pick the voice that suits your archetype(s) best. Each archetype is associated with a certain brand voice. For the sake of simplicity, I have collapsed the various brand voices under four main voices.

Archetype	Brand voice should sound relatively...
Outlaw	Technical
Magician	Technical
Hero	Technical
Lover	Casual
Jester	Casual
Everyman	Simple
Caregiver	Simple
Ruler	Formal
Creator	Technical
Innocent	Simple
Sage	Formal
Explorer	Casual

Step 2.6.3.7: Maintain consistency. Once you've decided on your brand voice, you must use it across all your social media postings and content created for the sake of consistency. Your brand voice will "speak" on your behalf, whether it be as text (in

the case of social media posts and website blogs) or as audio (in the case of videos and podcasts).

Step 2.6.4: Craft your brand values

Now, brand values are something that are both implicit and explicit at the same time. They are implicit in the sense that they're not "in the face" of the audience. The audience tries to discern what your values are by referring to other components of your brand persona. This is quite unlike your brand name, brand slogan and brand voice, which are much clearer indicators of your brand persona. As an implicit component of the brand persona, you don't have to worry so much about maintaining this. Maintaining the rest of the other components will carry this along. The explicit part about brand values is that sometimes you may wish to explicitly mention them on your website, just like how organisations do under the "About" section of their website.

Now, with that in mind, let's craft our brand values. To do so, we need to think about how society expects each archetype to behave.

Why are we referring to society's expectations? Because people have always attached expectations of behaviour to the characters they encounter in stories. Whenever we read of a "vizier" in Middle Eastern folk tales, we always expect the vizier to be evil. Whenever we read of a "maiden" in European folk tales, we always expect the maiden to be delicate and gentle. Over time, our collective minds have collated these characters into archetypes. And these expected behaviours have been

Step 2: Craft Your Brand Persona

collated into expected values. After all, behaviour is driven by values. One would not "destroy" (behaviour) if one didn't hold the value of "destruction". One would not "empathise" (behaviour) if one didn't hold the value of "empathy". So let's take a look at what these expected values are.

Archetype	Brand values should be
Outlaw	Pseudo-aggression and rebellion
Magician	Fantasy and mystery
Hero	Protection and strength
Lover	Sensuality and intimacy
Jester	Playfulness and humour
Everyman	Politeness and hospitality
Caregiver	Care and empathy
Ruler	Control and authority
Creator	Innovation and novelty
Innocent	Purity and virtuousness
Sage	Wisdom and guidance
Explorer	Courage and adventure

Now, as per the previous exercises, if we had chosen more than one archetype, we would then amalgamate the values of the chosen archetypes. So, for example, if we wanted our personal brand to be based upon the Sage and Explorer archetypes, our brand values would then be "wisdom, guidance, courage and adventure". Accordingly, thus, society would expect us to be wise, guiding, courageous and adventurous.

Step 2.6.5: Flip your values around to see your anti-values

Now, what are our brand anti-values? They're the opposite of what our values are. They're what society expects us not to hold, and accordingly, not to behave as. For our personal branding purposes, they serve as brand limits or perimeters. Should we find ourselves stepping outside of those limits, we will know that we have gone off-brand. Now, we won't be posting these anti-values anywhere. They will always remain implicit, but we must be cognizant of them, so that we can maintain our behaviour within our brand limits. So let's see what the anti-values are in relation to the brand values above.

Archetype	Brand values should be	Brand anti-values are
Outlaw	Pseudo-aggression and rebellion	Harmony and obedience
Magician	Fantasy and mystery	Practicality and reality
Hero	Protection and strength	Harm and weakness
Lover	Sensuality and intimacy	Frigidity and disengagement
Jester	Playfulness and humour	Seriousness and formality
Everyman	Politeness and hospitality	Rudeness and exclusion
Caregiver	Care and empathy	Inattention and indifference
Ruler	Control and authority	Disorganisation and subordination
Creator	Innovation and novelty	Tradition and stagnation

Step 2: Craft Your Brand Persona

Innocent	Purity and virtuousness	Carnality and immorality
Sage	Wisdom and guidance	Ignorance and neglect
Explorer	Courage and adventure	Cowardice and inactivity

If you wanted to be known as a Sage, but you demonstrate ignorance on your subject matter expertise, or if you neglect helping others along, you'd be going off-brand. Similarly, if you wanted to be known as a Creator but you stick very closely to tried and tested methods in your subject matter area, or if you're not informed about the recent developments in that area, you're not being very creatorly.

Step 2.6.6: Visualise your brand visual identity

Seeing is believing. Pictures paint a thousand words. All that cliched jazz. Essentially, your brand visual identity will paint a picture of your persona.

Now, what is the visual identity composed of? Anything that represents your brand visually, really, from a logo to your website to photos posted on social media to social media banners to videos. Now, there's two different methods here in creating your visual identity. One method is for the logo, while the other method is for all other visual identity.

Let's take a look at your logo first. Now, this is completely optional. There are many professionals who do not have a logo, and they're doing fine. If you choose to have a logo, here's what you need to know.

There are three kinds of logo that you can consider. The

first is a typographical logo. The second is a symbol logo. The third is a word art logo.

A typographical logo is simply your name and/or brand name written in a certain typeface. In the days of non-digital design, when hand lettering was still an important aspect of graphic design, typography was looked at in a very exacting manner. Typographers would pay really close attention to the anatomy of the letters in fonts. They would pay very close attention to the relationship between letters, such as in the kerning, leading and tracking. These days, with digital design, the importance of typography has waned a fair bit. Today, the general principles of typography are:

- A serif font (a font with projections coming out of letters) tends to look classic and distinguished.
- A serif font (a font with no projections coming out of letters) tends to look modern and contemporary.
- A script font (a font written in a cursive sort of way) tends to have a handwritten, casual feel.
- A display font (a font with eccentric designs) tends to be pretty, but difficult to read for anything more than short phrases.

I'm saying this in a very general way. For example, "Old English", which is a serif font, has been used in a lot of urban, ghetto and gangster designs. In this usage, it is far from classic and distinguished. It, rather, represents grit, strength and brotherhood.

Step 2: Craft Your Brand Persona

For all practical purposes, the only thing you need to know in choosing a suitable font is that different fonts have different connotations to them based on how they have been used by others before you. These connotations may be both positive and negative. "Impact" has been used in memes since the early days of Web 2.0. It is now associated with boldness, strength and wit. On the other hand, "Comic Sans" has been used so excessively since the days of Web 1.0 that it feels overused and immature. For your case, therefore, choose a font that has as close a connotation to your chosen archetype.

A symbol logo is a logo that represents your brand through the use of abstract shapes. Now, if you wanted a symbol logo for yourself, how would you go about doing it? First, take a look at the symbols and products that are associated with your subject matter area. Next, choose one of them and try to put your personal twist on it. Thus, a blockchain developer might choose a network diagram as his personal logo. A jazz or classical musician might choose an F-hole as his personal logo. A DJ might choose a turntable or headphones or an alien head as his personal logo. (Graphic design students do learn a whole lot more about logo design, such as "golden ratio", the principle of balance and the principle of movement, but for your case as a non-designer, I think this should suffice.)

A word art logo simply is when you turn your real name or brand name into a symbol that represents your subject matter area. It is effectively a combination of the two logo types above.

Now, what about photos, videos, banners and all the other stuff that also make up your visual identity? You would need to be aware of the "look and feel" of these photos, videos and banners used by other professionals or companies in your subject matter area (representing your core archetype) and then add your own little twist to it (based on your influencer archetype). General rules for each archetype can be seen below:

Archetype	Photos, banners and videos should look...
Outlaw	Combative and rebellious against the norms
Magician	Fantastical and mysterious
Hero	Protective and strong
Lover	Sensual and intimate
Jester	Playful and humorous
Everyman	Polite and welcoming
Caregiver	Caring and empathetic
Ruler	Commanding and authoritative
Creator	Innovative and always with fresh ideas
Innocent	Unassuming and child-like
Sage	Wise and guiding
Explorer	Intrepid and bold

Just as it is with your brand voice, you would need to maintain this visual expression consistently across all the platforms where your personal brand is present. For platforms that you use for your private side, such as your Discord server or Telegram channel, you don't have to maintain this visual expression.

Step 2: Craft Your Brand Persona

Step 2.6.7: Craft a brand vision

Just like brand values and anti-values, the brand vision is both implicit and explicit at the same time. You're not going to mention it to every person you meet all the time.

"Hi! I'm Jacob! I intend to be the most disruptive tech entrepreneur on the planet!"

No. It's implicit because the audience will try to guess your vision through the other components of your brand persona. Generally, if they see that your brand persona is poorly developed or not convincing, they will think that your brand vision is not all that ambitious. On the reverse, if they see that you have a very developed brand persona, they will think that your brand vision is highly ambitious.

It is explicit because you might wish to write it on your website, just like how organisations do under the "About" section of their website.

For your own purposes though, it helps you set a goal for your mastery of your area of competency. Previously in the chapter on competency, we spoke about setting goals to develop your competency. We also spoke about developing mastery in your subject matter area through applying your knowledge and skills. Now, setting a brand vision helps you set goals for that mastery.

There are different levels of mastery that you can aim for. If we take a look at taekwondo, for example, the masteries stretch from the 4th dan black belt to the 9th dan black belt, and it takes years of practice to move up the dan ranks.

Craft your personal brand vision in a sentence that specifies what you want to achieve within a time horizon. For your own purposes, set your brand vision vis-a-vis a target audience. If you eventually want to be the expert among experts, you would need to reach the pinnacle of mastery. If you only want to be an expert among beginners, you would not need to reach such a high level of mastery. Your personal brand vision may read something like this: "To become the industry leader in web3 digital marketing serving smart contract developers and NFT creators by 2035". This certainly reads like the professional is aiming for a very high level of mastery.

Or it could read something like this: "To become a mentor to beginner NFT creators by 2025". This certainly reads like the professional is aiming for a rather low level of mastery. And that's okay. There is no right or wrong when it comes to our preferences for a level of mastery and a target audience. I know people who stand at the apex of their subject matter areas and have chosen deeper mastery and lesser breadth. I also know people who are lesser masters but have more than one subject matter area of expertise.

Step 2.6.8: Craft a brand mission

Your brand mission is highly visible to others. Although you do not need to declare your mission, your actions will speak for themselves. The audience will judge your brand mission through the activities that you undertake as an industry professional with a personal brand. The activities that you undertake as a professional will also subsequently factor into your brand storytelling. They will become part of your plot.

Step 2: Craft Your Brand Persona

Your brand mission helps you stay on track of your brand vision. It helps you focus on the activities that would drive you closer with each step towards your objectives. Consider the following scenarios:

Judy plans to be a B2B marketer in the tech space. She sees the value of livestreaming and wants to make it a mainstream channel for e-commerce platforms, social media platforms and other businesses to engage their customers. Judy didn't really plot out her mission well. She took some jobs in sales, and then she took up a teaching assistant job for a while, and now she's in an administrative role. She's not likely to reach the objective she set for herself. Accordingly, she's not going to be able to tell a good brand story with these activities.

Jaida plans to be a B2B marketer in the tech space. She sees the value of livestreaming and wants to make it a mainstream channel for e-commerce platforms, social media platforms and other businesses to engage their customers. Jaida plotted out her mission quite well. She started off working in sales for a small tech startup. When that startup failed, she moved on to another job in the media sector. She worked as a production assistant for a while, where she learnt the ropes of video pre-production, production and post-production. She tied the knowledge she gained to the product knowledge she gained from working with the startup earlier. When Jaida left the production house, she signed up for a course in digital marketing. She read deeper into some concepts that were only tangentially mentioned during the course, such as a "sales canvas", "business model canvas" and "sales script". She felt that she needed to know this in order to see further the differences between a B2C and a B2B market. Jaida felt she was ready to tackle the B2B tech market. She looked for tech companies that primarily served B2B clients and were hiring for sales or marketing roles. Jaida is well on her way to reaching her horizon. She can tell a pretty sweet brand story with the activities that she has undertaken so far.

Taking stock

In this chapter, we looked at crafting your own brand persona. Your brand persona should come after developing your competencies. This is because as a professional, your competencies are your foundation. Without competencies, a brand persona won't do much for your personal brand. Furthermore, only after developing competencies can you discover the intricacies which would help you develop your brand persona.

In crafting your brand persona, I first advised you to renounce the employee mindset. It is not that we're trying to be disloyal to our companies here. We're not. We're just allowing ourselves to tap into a larger set of resources from the industry rather than a smaller set of resources from within our organisations of employment.

We then used the "deeper reaper" method to depersonify ourselves and repersonify ourselves again. We need to depersonify ourselves in order to clearly separate our professional side and private side. We need to do this because among many things, we don't want our private side to negatively affect our professional side in this era of "the many watching the many".

Step 2: Craft Your Brand Persona

We repersonify ourselves by choosing archetypes. These archetypes would form the basis of the personas that we would be creating for ourselves. It is important for us to choose a core archetype that is similar to other professionals with our subject matter expertise. We additionally can choose an influencer archetype that we're comfortable in carrying. The core and influencer archetypes should then be amalgamated to form our brand personality.

Our brand personality then has to be expressed coherently through several components, namely, our brand name, our brand slogan, our brand voice, our brand values and anti-values, our brand visual identity, our brand vision and our brand mission.

Our brand name should be able to demonstrate our subject matter expertise, distinguish ourselves from other professionals and fit our chosen archetype(s).

Our brand slogan should be written as a quotation so that it can be used in a sentence seamlessly. This helps us gain brand recall among members of the market and industry.

Our brand voice, composed of the lexicon and grammar, could be written in a formal, technical, casual or simple way. Each of these four ways corresponds to a fit with all the archetypes discussed. This brand voice is going to be used whenever we post on social media or create content.

Our brand values are what society expects our archetypes to hold. In relation to that are the anti-values, which are what society expects each archetype not to hold. Should we behave in a way that demonstrates the anti-values of our archetype, as opposed to our values, it would seem jarring, and create a sense of cognitive dissonance among the audience. For our purposes, crafting anti-values helps us stay on brand.

Our brand visual identity is how we present our brand visually to the public. We visually communicate our brand persona through the logo, photos and videos that we post on our websites and social media. These, again, should fit the archetypes that we have chosen as the basis of our brand personas.

The brand vision helps us set our goals for mastering our subject matter areas. Through applying our knowledge and skills in our subject matter areas, we are moving in the step of mastery. Now, which level of mastery do we want to reach? We can just be lower-level masters, or we can be higher-level masters. It all depends on how we craft our goals through our brand vision.

Finally, our brand mission helps us set the plot to our brand stories. It helps us set our sights on our brand vision and craft the steps we need to take to reach it.

In the next chapter, we will look at how we use storytelling to tell our personal brand stories. I will revisit the plot structures and modes of persuasion we covered earlier and explain how we, too, can craft our brand stories.

CHAPTER 7

Step 3: (Re)tell Your Story

So we've developed our competencies and crafted our brand personas. We now need to stitch our experiences together to tell a coherent brand story. The audience does not see professionals "in the moment". The audience wants to know the (hi)story of the professional. They want to see what brought the professional to where he is. What has he experienced? What has he learnt? Is he competent enough for their needs? Is the persona just a mirage or does it really hold water?

The story is the packaging for your personal brand. The design of your packaging can seriously influence how the market and industry see your brand. Should your brand contain no packaging, the audience will only be able to see your competencies and your persona. With the packaging, they will be able to tell how the competencies and the persona are related to each other.

The intended target audience must be convinced of the story. This is why we use the method of storytelling to create a convincing story. What we're doing is that we're appealing to the human mind's proclivity towards familiar plot moulds, and combining it with modes of persuasion to get the plot across in a more convincing narrative. So let's begin crafting our stories.

We're going to go through four steps. The first step requires you to structure your brand story into three parts. You would need to tell how you began developing your chosen competency, the milestones and highlights of your career so far, where you are currently and where you plan to be in the future. You would then need to decide what to do with your former personal brand. You have a choice as to whether to incorporate it, retire it or hibernate it. Guidance will be provided on the choices you could consider making. You would then need to modify your brand story with an archetypal plot. The choice entirely depends on what you wish to highlight, and whether or not you have the prerequisites to use that archetypal plot. Examples will be given on who might be more inclined to use certain archetypal plots. Finally, you will add some modes of persuasion to spice up your story. Guidance will be given on how to use each mode of persuasion.

Step 3.1: Apply a three-act structure

The three-act structure is the most basic of all plot structures and can be found almost everywhere, in every piece of music we

Step 3: (Re)tell Your Story

hear, every movie we watch. It is the most diminutive division of storytelling upon which more complex narratives are built. In writing a three-act structure, we will first craft an explanation of how our personal brand began. In other words, what spurred us to develop the competencies we chose. Here, we need to mention whether we developed those competencies through formal means, or we gained mastery through experience on the ground, or a combination of both. I recommend having a combination of both to support the domain authority that we have in that subject matter. If you had gone through formal means of learning, couple that with some mention about experience gained on the ground. If you have picked up the skills through learning from experience, go ahead and get some certifications from affordable sources such as Udemy, Coursera or any of the other online learning platforms. You can also check if Google or any other organisations offer free certifications in those areas.

Next, we need to make mention of the most interesting things that have happened ever since we've been championing this brand. This will be the part that speaks the loudest. This is where you again drop the names of major clients or speak of your greatest achievements.

Finally, we need to resolve the story with a soft ending. We need to mention where we are at the moment and where we are heading to next. We're not going to end with a hard ending because, hey, we ain't dead yet. We need to leave some space for the plot to be extended in the future. It's kind of like the classic "And they lived happily ever after" ending that we hear after almost every European folk tale we've ever encountered (interestingly enough, tales from the Americas such as Brer Rabbit or stories of frontiersmen don't feature such endings).

Everyone with a strong personal brand has a brand story to back his brand up. If you have ever listened to any stories of entrepreneurs over TED Talks or the infamous Fuckup Nights (I say this in the most endearing of manners), you will find this three-act structure used in every single story. "Hi, I'm Judd. I founded a company at age.... Little did I know that I was going to lose everything I ever worked hard for... Now, I am..."

Now try this:

1. Write a couple of sentences about how you started on the path to developing that area of competency. Do mention the training that you undertook, whether it be formal or through self-directed means. Also mention the activities you took to apply your learning (refer to the chapter on developing competencies).
2. Write a couple of sentences about the milestones and highlights of your career so far. Now, remember, you should only mention older milestones and highlights of your former personal brand if you are incorporating it into your current brand. If you are retiring or hibernating it, you should avoid making mention of older milestones and highlights. More details on this in Step 3.2.
3. Write a couple of sentences about where you are now, and where you want to be in the future.

Step 3: (Re)tell Your Story

Step 3.2: Decide what to do with your former brand

Now, this step is only necessary for professionals who are rebranding. For those who are creating their first brand, please feel free to skip this step.

Now, if you're rebranding, you would have had a former brand that you're branding away from. You have three options as to what to do with that brand. You can incorporate that brand into your story, retire it or keep it in hibernation. This decision will also lead you to your next step where you would modify your brand story with an archetypal plot.

Decision	Reason	Archetypal plot choices
Incorporate	Our former brand can flow smoothly into and can add value to our new brand	· Overcoming the Monster · Rebirth · Rags to Riches · Tragedy · Comedy
Retire	Our former brand is going to negatively affect our current brand.	· Quest · Journey and Return
Hibernate	We cannot as yet make sense of how to use it in our new personal brands	· Quest · Journey and Return

Once you've made your decision as to what to do with your former personal brand, move on to Step 3.

Step 3.3: Modify the story with an archetypal plot

Think of this as the next step in dramatisation. Every story needs some drama. How interesting would a story about dorks doing dorky stuff exclusively be? Computers! Board games! Computers! Board games! End. How interesting would a story about jocks doing jocky stuff exclusively be? Sports! Beer! Sports! Beer! End. Neither story would be an interesting story at all.

But which archetypal plot should you choose? Let's use the guide below:

Archetypal Plot	Use this…	Prerequisite	Usually used by
Overcoming the Monster	If you wish to highlight that your strength lies in your ability to overcome major challenges	There must have been a major challenge that you went through, conquered and emerged stronger from	Professionals who have gone through a major disruption to their professional lives
Rebirth	If you wish to highlight that you made some mistakes in the past but now you have changed and are ready to take on a fully professional persona	There must have been a mistake you made in the past. There must be evidence that you have changed.	Professionals who have had brushes with the law Professionals who have misspent their times in extravagant luxury
Quest	If you wish to highlight that you are resourceful and dare tread where others don't	You must have developed competencies in a subject matter that is specialised, niche or rare	Professionals who are deeply specialised in a certain subject matter

Step 3: (Re)tell Your Story

Journey and Return	If you wish to highlight that you took a sabbatical for professional reasons and came back with fresh, new ideas	You must have taken a sabbatical. You must be better at your profession now than you were in the past.	Professionals who changed between unrelated careers
Rags to Riches	If you wish to highlight that despite your less than privileged past, you have managed to scale yourself up	You must have a huge contrast between your conditions in the past and your conditions now	Professionals who are "self made".
Tragedy	If you wish to garner sympathy from the audience	You must have had pretty severely unfortunate experiences in your professional life	Professionals who just need a job to get back on their feet
Comedy	If you wish to show positivity above all else	You must have a way to see the bright side of everything	Professionals who need to approach an audience who prioritise positivity

Try rewriting the brand story you wrote in Step 1 using the archetypal plot that you chose in Step 3.

Step 3.4: Add some persuasive spice

So now you've chosen a suitable pot. You've thrown all the ingredients in. It's time to add some spice. These spices are used to appeal to the audience. You may wish to use just one spice, some of them or all of them at once. It depends on what you're trying to achieve. Let's see the guide below.

Mode of persuasion	Use this if you want to appeal to...	How to use it
Ethos	Your own authority as a professional	Find somewhere in your brand story to insert the phrase, "As a [insert profession], I am all for / convinced that / adamant that / supportive of..."
Pathos	The emotions of the audience	Replace words with synonyms that have a more emotional connotation
Logos	The logical side of the audience	Find somewhere in your brand story where there is a cause and an effect. Insert the phrase, "If [insert details of the cause], then logically [insert details of the effect]..."
Kairos	The similarity between your story and current affairs	Find somewhere in your brand story that has a similarity with whatever is happening in current affairs. Insert the phrase, "[insert details of your experience], just like [insert details of current affairs]."
Topos	The tone of voice of the audience instead of your own brand voice	Rewrite your story to sound more formal, technical, casual or simple, depending on the tone of voice of the audience.

Now, take the rewrite you did in Step 3, and reword some parts of it with the spices above. At the end of this exercise, your story will not only be able to package your competencies and brand persona well, it will also be memorable.

Step 3: (Re)tell Your Story

Taking stock

Storytelling as a method uses the familiar components of stories that we've grown to become familiar with, and applied to information that we wish to relay in a memorable, easy to understand way. Here, we have applied it to personal branding, where our brand story serves as the packaging for our competencies and brand personas.

In this chapter, we have looked at mapping our brand stories into a structure for easy consumption. We have also looked at what to do with our former personal brands, which then leads us to a selection of choices of archetypal plots. We then chose these archetypal plots based on our needs, and applied the modes of persuasion for added appeal.

After completing this step, your personal (re)brand is now complete. You can now (re)tell your story. You can update your resumes and LinkedIn "About" sections with this story, and can also (re)tell it during interviews or first meetings with clients and collaborators. Keep it handy. You will need it.

CHAPTER 8

Step 4: Optimising Your Personal Brand

Hang on.

Just because you've developed your competencies, crafted your brand persona and drafted your brand story, doesn't mean it's the end of your personal brand journey. The personal branding project does not have an end. You need to constantly optimise your personal brand so that you can reap its benefits constantly. By optimising your personal brand, you will be able to gain a competitive advantage over other professionals. You will also be able to stay relevant in the market and industry. There will be threats around, especially in this digital age of "the many watching the many". You will be in a good position to mitigate these threats. Should any major shocks to the industry occur, you would have built up some resilience to come

Step 4: Optimising Your Personal Brand

back even stronger. Finally, by optimising your personal brand, you're sending a clear signal to the market and industry, and will subsequently be able to find a good fit between your brand persona and the personality of your potential employers, clients or collaborators. In short, by optimising your personal brand, you are only making it stronger.

We can borrow two important concepts from systems thinking to conceptualise the need for optimisation here. In systems thinking, we recognise that the actions of various people in an organisation can either create a "balancing loop" or a "reinforcing loop". A balancing loop is where the organisation's interest is to stabilise itself. A new organisation will suffer from a "liability of newness" according to organisational ecologists. It needs to stabilise itself. An organisation that has cash flow issues needs to stabilise itself to maintain liquidity in the next 12 months and maintain solvency beyond that.

A reinforcing loop is where the organisation's interest is to progress. Organisations which just had an infusion of capital would need to progress in order to meet the targets set by the capital investors. Organisations riding on a bull market, too, need to progress to capitalise on the upward trend.

It's kind of like a person riding a bicycle. At lower speeds, or when there is a danger of collision, the rider will be focused on stabilising his bicycle. At higher speeds or when the road ahead is clear, the rider will be focused on moving forward.

Now, what does this have to do with personal branding? At times, you might need to stabilise your personal brand. This especially happens when you've just recently crafted this brand,

and need the market and industry to take you seriously as an industry professional. This might happen if you've just graduated and this is your first personal brand, or if you've recently rebranded. Brand refreshes generally don't need such stability, because it follows the stability of the existing brand.

At other times, you might need to progress your personal brand. This especially happens when you've been championing the brand for a while, and now need to develop the brand further. You may see the need to go into deeper levels of mastery in the subject area, or to adopt new complementary competencies. You may see the need to strengthen your brand persona in order to reach out more effectively to potential employers, clients or collaborators. Or you may see the need to make amendments to your brand story, adding new milestones or updating your future plans.

Whether you're stabilising your brand, or progressing it forward, optimisation is going to be useful for your needs. So here's what you need to do to optimise your personal brand.

There will be three actions that I will discuss here. These actions are in no specific order. First, you need to pay attention to the developments in the market and industry. The market is a fickle mistress. And the industry supports its wants and needs no matter what. You may need to develop complementary competencies to adapt to market needs. You may need to remap these competencies into a hierarchy based on what the market prioritises for the moment. At the end of the day, you should use signals from the market to inform you as to whether you need to simply update yourself, refresh your brand or to rebrand.

Step 4: Optimising Your Personal Brand

Second, you need to update your digital presence. The world is increasingly digital. Since ARPANET became the internet around 1995, the world has adopted more and more digitisation. Your digital presence is more important today than it has ever been. Update your personal brand's digital footprint. Keep the digital accounts of your personal brand open to the public. Keep the digital accounts of your private life guarded. Not everyone is able to merge their private lives with their professional lives, as I have mentioned many times in this book.

Thirdly, watch out for threats. There are three kinds of threats to your professional career. Respond with immediate urgency to threats which are urgent. Keep an eye out for threats which are proximal and try to remove yourself from them. Always be on the lookout for threats which are dormant. You never know when they'll surface.

Action 1: Keep your eye on the market and industry

Markets will change. So will industries. Markets have wants and needs, and we need to respond to these wants and needs. Most importantly, we need to address the pain points of the market, and hopefully be able to give some additional gains too. As markets change, industries will too. The market is the demand, while industries are the supply, after all.

How will this change occur? At times there will be minor changes, but at other times there will be major changes. A new professional software might be introduced in the market, which requires us as professionals to upskill ourselves to learn it. When TikTok introduced three new features in 2022, including

TikTok paid marketing, TikTok gifting and TikTok Stories, every professional whose profession was affected by this change – including digital marketers, data scientists, UI/UX designers and content creators – scrambled to learn how these new features could be used effectively for their professional purposes. They didn't just learn the features. They learnt how the features were being used and projected the potential impact these features could have for their employers, clients and collaborators. Of course, they looked at different aspects of the new features, The digital marketers looked at how the new features affected organic marketing and the potential of lead generation, The UI/UX designers looked at how the new features affected human-computer interaction as well as if those new features could be replicated on other platforms, and the data scientists looked at the algorithm engine for recommendations on the "For You page". In 2022, too, many companies started replacing the term "human resource management" with "people management". This was done in response to recognising that employees weren't just resources to be used by organisations, but rather human beings who would perform better as employees if their needs were accounted for. This, of course, required a mindset change among human resource practitioners. Companies which didn't have strong hiring policies and practices undoubtedly had trouble adopting this new mindset.

At other times, there will be more major changes. Take a look at the scenario below.

Jon was a self-dubbed "early internet guru". As soon as dial-up connectivity hit his town, Jon was already experimenting

Step 4: Optimising Your Personal Brand

with it. He bought books on Hypertext Markup Language (HTML). He bought homepage asset kits, which, at the time, consisted of GIFs and wallpapers. He learned how to code in HTML on his own. He knew his way around the architecture of websites. All his friends looked to him to develop their websites. He had his own website, a fansite for his favourite band, The Doors. There he shared short streaming video clips of their interviews as well as some rare music through a plugin from RealMedia. Pretty soon, Jon was employed by a dot-com company as a website developer. Not through his educational training but through his sheer experience and self-taught expertise. The dot-com bubble burst around the mid-2000s and Jon was left out of a job. Jon felt a little disheartened at this and left the IT industry. He found a job in hospitality, which was what he was formally trained in after he left high school. Jon spent several years in the hospitality industry, quite happy to move around from the banquet team to the rooms team to the reception team. One day, Jon attended a free IT seminar where all these new terms were thrown around. He discovered new things about the internet that he had never heard of before when he was knee-deep in it years ago. Ron felt motivated to go back to web development. He prepared his resume and his portfolio and Googled for jobs in web development. "Google, haha," thought he. "Whatever happened to Altavista?" To Jon's surprise, he could not understand the job descriptions or job requirements that he found. HTML alone was not enough. Web developers now had to work with Cascading Style Sheets and JavaScript. And what in the world did "responsive design" mean anyway? He was also surprised to hear that web developers weren't the heroes they were in the past. They now were part of a larger team, including UI/UX designers and search engine optimisation (SEO) digital marketers. These were major changes in the industry which Jon was not privy to.

Certainly, the market is going to continue remapping skillsets needed to perform certain roles. Decades ago, the business world declared that professionals could no longer be specialists or generalists. They needed to have "T-shaped skills", which meant that they needed to have one skill that they specialised in (the vertical stroke of the T) and one generic skill (the horizontal stroke). Soon after, many industries realised that T-shaped skills weren't enough. Many professionals were now required to have two specialised skills, leaking to the term "pi-shaped skills". And then more and more skillsets were required, leading to the term "comb-shaped skills".

Eventually, you too would have to develop many skills as an industry professional. Most of these skills would be complementary stalls related to the primary competency that you developed. Product managers were once, many years ago, just product managers. Eventually, they had to pick up skills in marketing too, so that they could bring their products to market. And once they began to work with larger and more cross-functional teams, they needed to pick up project management skills too. In the beginning, they just needed to know how to manage product development projects in the traditional or "waterfall" style. With the increasing popularity of lean organisational structures, they also needed to learn "agile" project management, where

Step 4: Optimising Your Personal Brand

short fortnightly sprints and daily scrums for the purpose of rapid prototyping would greatly benefit the lean organisation. Every other profession in the world has experienced this same fate as well. Professionals in that industry have had to adopt complementary skills as time went by in order to stay relevant and perform their roles effectively. This is going to continue well into the future, with the business environment changing at an ever-increasingly rapid pace.

When you have developed several complementary skillsets in relation to your chosen role as an industry professional, do take note that you might need to place these skillsets into a hierarchy. In other words, what should you be known first and foremost as? What should you be known secondarily as? What should you be known tertiarily as? The choice will be dictated largely by the market. Whatever the market is in the mood for, for the season, should be your "first read". This is a term used in industrial design to denote the part of the design that the audience sees first of all. Your personal brand is by your design. You, and only you, can direct which skillsets should be the first, second and third reads. If, let's say, you've developed skills in logistics, e-commerce and management, what should the public see first? Should the public see you as a logistics specialist who happens to work in e-commerce and is in a managerial role? Or should the public see you as an e-commerce specialist who has a background in logistics and is managing a warehouse? Or should the public see you as an experienced manager of e-commerce ventures who has strengths in logistics?

So how do we keep our eye on the market and industry?

Instead of mindlessly scrolling our private social media feed and stories looking at pictures of babies and whatnot, scroll through LinkedIn. Instead of watching old music videos over and over again on YouTube, watch educational content instead. There are a variety of content creators in your chosen subject matter area, many of whom will regularly update, analyse and review changes in the market and industry. Sign in to your favourite job portal and sign up for push notifications.

Then we take note of these changes. Don't ignore them. If you do, these changes will turn into threats. While some of these changes might just be a flash in the pan, others may really take root in the market and industry. When they do, they will no longer be threats at that point. They will become real issues, and your inability to respond to them will become your weakness. Too many times I've met baby boomers who are unable to perform basic computer operations in this day and age. And they always have the same excuse: "Oh, I'm not used to doing this. My staff usually does the computer work for me."

If you were to find a way to respond to these changes, you will turn them instead into opportunities. Capitalising on these opportunities will benefit you because it adds on to your strengths. Having these strengths not only help you stay relevant, it will also allow you to seamlessly refresh your brand.

In short, when changes are minor but your skills are still aligned with market wants and needs, update yourself with the changes.

When changes are minor but there is a slight misalignment with market wants and needs, refresh your brand.

Step 4: Optimising Your Personal Brand

When changes are major and you can't effectively serve the market anymore, or if the market disappears, leaving you with skills that no one is willing to pay for, rebrand.

Action 2: Update your digital presence

People Google other people's names all the time. Whenever you are introduced to a new client or collaborator, or when you submit a job application, one of the first things that the potential client, collaborator or employer will do is to Google you.

This is why you need to update your digital presence.

Tip 1: Constantly come back to your LinkedIn page, online portfolio or anywhere else where your personal brand has a digital footprint:

- Make sure every single text post, graphic, photo or video there is aligned with your brand persona. Refer to the brand visual identity and brand voice that you crafted to remind you.
- Make sure that all your certifications and accomplishments are up to date. Your audience wants to see developments in your brand story. They want to see how far you have progressed as an indication of where you will go in the future. Your audience will see your career in the manner of Isaac Newton's first law of motion: A body at rest tends to stay at rest; a body in motion tends to stay in motion.
- You may choose to reshuffle your competencies into a hierarchy in relation to market trends. Accordingly,

you may wish to make minor changes to your brand persona and brand story to reflect this reshuffled hierarchy.
- Remove any text post, graphic, photo or video that is not in line with your brand story. If you had done a certification in massage therapy at some point in time, but you're not currently promoting yourself as a massage therapist, remove that certification. Too much clutter will confuse the audience. Keep that certification in hibernation. You have earned it, but doesn't mean you need to show it.
- Create a couple of pieces of professional content to demonstrate your mastery. Post a LinkedIn article about your ruminations on your subject matter area. Upload an infographic about your thought processes in designing or programming. You don't need to post frequently, unless you're a content creator. As an industry professional, a couple of insightful pieces every six months should suffice.

Tip 2: Keep the digital accounts of your personal brand open to the public. If you let your audience see what they want to see, they are likely to be satisfied and not search any further. This is what we call the principle of "satisficing" in behavioural economics. As long as people adequately find what they set out to find, they will not be motivated to continue the search. If they don't find what they set out to find, they will look further. And guess what? Everybody has a skeleton or two in their closet.

Step 4: Optimising Your Personal Brand

I was once living in an area where drug addicts used to break into people's cars. They'd steal stuff from parked cars in order to fund their drug lifestyles. So how did we address this problem? We'd deliberately open our glove compartments to show that there is nothing to steal. The addicts then wouldn't bother breaking into our cars and move along, looking for another opportunity.

Tip 3: Keep the digital accounts of your private life guarded. You never know who might find your private life objectionable. Remember, even in a society of saints there will still be sinners. I once was involved in an industry network where the word "sexy" was just about the most common adjective used. It was used to refer to anything that was appealing. In that network, a cufflink could be "sexy". An ergonomic mouse could be "sexy". I suppose the word "sexy" itself was "sexy". Yet, the fine folks at TikTok do not share that same opinion. Just using that word alone in hashtags could get one flagged. And Facebook is going in that direction too. So you see, the very idea of "objectionable" is vague. Don't let that vagueness be an impediment to your personal brand.

Action 3: Watch out for threats

Refer back to the SWOT analysis you did when you were deciding on a competency. What were the threats you identified?

Now, reassess them after your (re)branding project is complete. Yes, as I will never tire of saying, the project is complete once you finish creating your brand story, but the journey is far from over. Categorise them into three types:

- Threats that are proximal
- Threats that are urgent
- Threats that are dormant

Proximal threats are threats that are really close to you. Imagine you're in the bathtub and there's a live wire just beside you. Yes, that's a proximal threat. Now, which threat in your professional life is proximal? It could be a bad manager who is known to blame others for his own faults. It could be a demanding client who threatens you with this and that. We've all met such threats in our professional life before. You need to keep your eye on proximal threats constantly. They can hit you at any time. I strongly recommend that you remove yourself from this threat. You have some reaction time here, so don't worry. The early warning indicator is visible but the trigger is not in sight yet. Which is something we can't say about the next category of threats.

Urgent threats are coming at you fast. You're a deer in the lights of a moving car. The trigger is visible and it's only a matter of time before you get hit. Move out of the way now. This kind of threats include news of your organisation of employment downsizing, or potential employers looking for new requirements that they didn't use to.

Dormant threats are always sitting there, lurking beneath the shadows. You know that they exist because of your prior experience. But you don't know if these threats are currently present. They may be there, or they may not be there. Threats of this manner include bad managers, poor application of

Step 4: Optimising Your Personal Brand

company protocols, procedures and policies, and colleagues who can negatively affect your working experience. They may not be visible to your naked eye now, but you know that these threats exist from hearing stories from other people, reading the news or even experiencing them yourself at previous jobs. At the expense of sounding negative, I strongly suggest that you tune your radar to and constantly watch out for these dormant risks manifesting themselves. Even if you have had a pleasurable experience to date, do not let your guard down, because situations can change for the worse. Sometimes the person you once knew will not be the same person you are going to get to know.

Taking stock

The industry professional doesn't exist in a vacuum. He always exists within an environment that can provide him with resources such as employment, career satisfaction and monetary reward. His competencies are his tools to obtain those resources. His brand persona constitutes his lodgings and clothing, protecting him from the elements while enabling him to use his tools to procure resources. His brand story is made up of all the smiles and scars he's collected over the years.

Does he need to maintain his tools? Sure he does. Knives get blunt after a while. Spears break. Nets tear. Does he need to maintain his lodgings and clothing? Sure he does. He needs to add more insulation for winter, and more ventilation for summer. Does he need to keep track of all the smiles and scars? Sure he does. They're all a part of him, for better or worse.

For these reasons, he needs to keep his eye on the market and industry. Markets are the demand for his competencies, and industries represent him and his fellow professionals. But markets will change. And accordingly, industries will change too. Sometimes there will be minor changes, but at other times the changes will be more major. He should firstly identify the changes to the market and industry by leveraging on online resources that will provide regular updates. He should secondly assess these changes to see what type and extent of action is needed of him. He must not ignore these changes. By ignoring these changes, he is inviting them to turn into threats. By responding to these changes, he is turning them into opportunities. He can then make the decision to either just update himself with the new changes, or to refresh his brand, or to rebrand.

Another action that he can undertake is to update his digital presence. He should constantly update his personal brand digital footprint with the latest developments in his career and ensure that everything that is visible to the public is aligned with his brand persona. He should also demonstrate his mastery of the subject area by creating content. Not as a full-fledged career content creator, but just enough to demonstrate that he has ruminated on the subject matter and he is confident of sharing his thoughts. As they say in digital marketing, "content is king". Meanwhile, he should keep his digital accounts associated with his personal brand open for the public to view, and keep his digital accounts associated with his private life closed tight.

Yet another action that he can undertake is to watch out for threats. Threats come in many forms, and safety should be

Step 4: Optimising Your Personal Brand

our number one priority. Some threats are right beside us. We can be affected just by being near them, but it doesn't mean that they're going to harm us. Some threats are coming for us, whether we like it or not. Some threats are hiding in the shadows. We need to move out of the way quickly for urgent threats, and always be on the look out for dormant threats.

I hope you keep up with these three tips. You have worked hard to build your personal brand. You now just need to maintain it.

CHAPTER 9

Not the End, but the Beginning

We have come to the end of this book, but I hope it's just the beginning of your journey to (re)brand yourself and (re)tell your story. I have primarily centred this book on three main concepts in personal branding. I have looked at brand persona, competencies and storytelling as the three pillars of your personal brand. These three components all have a theoretical grounding to them, which I have delved into. The brand persona is based on concepts used in organisational branding, which I have adapted into personal branding. I have looked at the 12 archetypes that are used in creating a brand personality, and further, I have shown how to create a brand persona from that brand personality.

Not the End, but the Beginning

Competency is a concept borrowed from instructional design. It is made up of knowledge, skills and attitude. But that is merely descriptive. In order to make it more actionable, I have extended that theoretical concept into "learn", "practice" and "apply", where learning enables you to obtain knowledge, practising enables you to develop skills and application enables you to work towards mastery.

Storytelling is a methodology that was theorised from grounded research into the stories that we all heard as children, and the stories that we continue to consume through books, movies and documentaries. I looked at the components of good storytelling, namely the basic three-act structure, the archetypal plots and the modes of persuasion.

Beyond these theoretical premises, I've given you an impetus as to why you should brand yourself. With a personal brand, you'll be able to gain a competitive edge over fellow professionals. Your brand persona will emphasise your competencies and your brand story will make your brand memorable. You will also be able to continually stay relevant in the industry, by keeping your eye on the developments in the market and industry. You will also be able to mitigate the risks of social media today, which is exacerbated by the culture of "blaming the offender" that is an unfortunate effect of the move towards equality. An industry professional with a personal brand is also equipped for resilience in the event of any shocks that might hit the industry. Your personal brand will also send a clear signal to the market and industry. You will be better able to conceptualise who your primary, secondary and target markets are. This will greatly help you in choosing who to work with, and also help the correct target market find you.

I have also placed personal branding on a timeline. I urge you to start your personal branding journey as early as possible, but it is never too late to start. Some of you might be branding yourself for the first time. Others might want to refresh their brand to correct tiny misalignments between what they can offer, and what the market needs. Some of you might be rebranding. I offered three options for those who are rebranding, as to what to do with their former personal brands. They could incorporate it, retire it, or hibernate it. At the end of the day, the industry professional should see himself as a house of brands. It is his duty, responsibility and prerogative to promote the brand that he wishes to be known by as a flagship brand, and to relegate some others as a side brand.

Step-by-step recommendations have also been provided for you to consider. I have advised that you first begin with competencies. Developing competencies should be your primary focus and priority in personal branding. I have gone through each step with you in developing your chosen competency. I have used the SWOT framework to recommend a way for you to identify your strengths, weaknesses, opportunities and threats. I have also adapted the BCG Matrix to help you analyse the trends in the market so that you can make better choices in deciding on a competency to develop. I then used three frameworks from user experience design to help you empathise with yourself. No one can understand what you think and feel better than you can. Once you've done all that, you will then identify

Not the End, but the Beginning

your performance gap with a simple set of questions that is often asked during "training needs analysis" sessions conducted by instructional designers. With this, you will go into the learning stage based on your learning preferences. You will then go into the practice stage using a reversed Bloom's Taxonomy, another framework from instructional design. Finally, you will begin your journey towards mastery by building a portfolio in the application stage.

    I then walked you through six steps in crafting a brand persona. These steps include changing your mindset from an "organisational employee" to an "industry professional", depersonifying yourself to separate your private life and professional life and subsequently repersonifying yourself to create a brand personality. I have gone through the brand archetypes again and the steps you need to take in order to choose an appropriate set of archetypes. The final step here is to develop the components of your brand persona, namely, your brand name, brand slogan, brand voice, brand values and anti-values, brand visual identity, brand vision and brand mission. All these components should be able to put an image upon your competencies, as well as to distinguish yourself from other industry professionals.

    I then walked you through the four steps in (re)telling your brand story. I have given you a structure composed of three parts to follow as a start. You would need to tell how you began developing your chosen competency, the milestones and highlights of your career so far, where you are currently and where you plan to be in the future. I then advised you to decide what to do with your former personal brand. You have a choice as to whether to incorporate it, retire it or hibernate it. Based on this decision, what you wish to highlight and your possession of certain prerequisites, you would then choose an archetypal plot and rewrite your story based on your choice of archetypal plot. And to make your story more persuasive, I have walked you through how to use the modes of persuasion.

At the end of this exercise, I have advised you to continue optimising your brand. You should conceptualise your brand as always in flux, because the market is always in flux. You are always either stabilising your brand, or progressing forward based on your market position. I have discussed three actions in this regard. You have been advised to pay attention to the developments in the market and industry. The market will dictate when you may need to develop complementary competencies. With these complementary competencies, you will need signals from the market to direct which of these skills you should put forward in order of importance. You will also be using market signals to tell you whether you need to simply update yourself, refresh your brand or to rebrand. I have also advised you to update your digital presence. Aside from keeping the digital accounts of your personal brand open to public, and the digital accounts of your private life guarded, I have walked you through some recommendations as to how to update your personal brand's digital footprint, including maintaining your brand visual identity and brand voice across all platforms and updating your digital footprint with the latest developments in your career. In my final note, I advised you to watch out for threats. As much as we want to believe in the good of others,

Not the End, but the Beginning

there is tons of evidence to show that threats do exist in the professional world. In this final note, I once again refer to the risk management framework to highlight three threats you should be aware of at all times.

The journey has just begun for you. Fare you well on your journey.

ABOUT THE AUTHOR

Dr Yasser Mattar is a practitioner and strong advocate of branding. As an experienced adult educator, academic product marketing manager and consultant, he has worked on multiple (re)branding exercises for enterprises as well as personal (re)branding exercises for individuals. His work has taken him to various countries around the world, most notably Australia, Singapore, Indonesia and the Philippines.

He himself is no stranger to personal branding, having successfully branded and rebranded six times in his career (thus far). Beginning his career as an economic sociologist, he rebranded himself next as an instructional designer, then as a startup/spinoff strategist, then as a project manager, then as a digital marketer and then as a visual communication designer. Threading all these brands together is the importance he places on education as well as on personal branding.

In his leisure time, he is currently working on an art project for the NFT/Metaverse space that reimagines feminine representations of the 12 animals of the Chinese zodiac.